THE
MYTHIC
WARRIOR'S
HANDBOOK

THE
MYTHIC WARRIOR'S
HANDBOOK

OUTSMART
ATHENA, SLAY MEDUSA,
IMPRESS ZEUS,
AND CLAIM YOUR PLACE
— IN —
THE PANTHEON OF THE GODS

WRITTEN BY CHIRON THE CENTAUR
TRANSLATED BY E. CARLSON AND H. DAY

AVON, MASSACHUSETTS

Published by
Adams Media, a division of F+W Media, Inc.
57 Littlefield Street, Avon, MA 02322. U.S.A.
www.adamsmedia.com

ISBN 10: 1-4405-0264-1
ISBN 13: 978-1-4405-0264-4

Printed in the United States of America.

10 9 8 7 6 5 4 3 2 1

Library of Congress Cataloging-in-Publication Data
is available from the publisher.

This publication is designed to provide accurate and authoritative information
with regard to the subject matter covered. It is sold with the understanding that
the publisher is not engaged in rendering legal, accounting, or other professional
advice. If legal advice or other expert assistance is required, the services of a com-
petent professional person should be sought.

—From a *Declaration of Principles* jointly adopted by a Committee of the
American Bar Association and a Committee of Publishers and Associations

Many of the designations used by manufacturers and sellers to distinguish their
product are claimed as trademarks. Where those designations appear in this book
and Adams Media was aware of a trademark claim, the designations have been
printed with initial capital letters.

Interior illustrations by Contact Jupiter / Claudia Wolf.

This book is available at quantity discounts for bulk purchases.
For information, please call 1-800-289-0963.

CONTENTS

TRANSLATORS' PREFACE TO THE HANDBOOK

Greek mythology has captured the hearts and enthralled the minds of generation after generation. The graphic violence. The bizarre love triangles. The hideous monsters. The stories of Greek heroes have entertained for ages. And now they're regarded as just that—stories. No truth, just make-believe. Even today's most enlightened scholars read the mythologies more like fiction than history. So did we. So did we. . . .

Our re-education in Greek mythology started one winter before school break. We were so busy grading papers we didn't realize there was a package at the bottom of the box where our students left their final assignments. The package was ordinary. (We actually thought it was more textbooks we couldn't afford.) It was the contents that were perplexing.

Inside was a letter from a benefactor, whose name we've been ordered not to reprint; it spoke of a long-forgotten tomb in a long-forgotten area of Greece and came with a map and directions written in Latin. At first we thought it was a joke, put together by another teacher's assistant escaping his own workload. But it was too detailed—even for the biggest procrastinator. After deciphering the whole thing, we realized this was the real deal. It was a map to the Tomb of Chiron—instructor of the great Greek heroes.

Now we're usually not that impulsive, but something about this grabbed us. We had to go to Greece. We had to follow the map. We had to see if the Tomb of Chiron was still there. So we did. (It was either that, or spend the rest of break ordering pizza and watching Netflix.)

With some "revising" of university paperwork, we were able to make this look like a legit trip. We were going to Greece to attend an academic conference and listen to a series of lectures by old guys in tweed blazers. We were *not* going to venture through the countryside, up steep mountains, and into dark caves. Nope. We never would've got funding for that.

A quick cross-reference with our modern-day oracle (aka Google) helped us update the map and directions. We knew the starting point was the city of Athens but we needed some help connecting that dot with the Tomb's location on Mt. Pelion, the one-time residence of Chiron the Centaur. Thank Zeus for Google Maps. We figured it'd be a three-day hike from the closest town. That is unless we ran into an angry Gorgon or bloodthirsty goat/snake/lion hybrid. We didn't. The only strange creatures we came across were a pack of stray cats. Easily vanquished by a can of tuna.

We were afraid the tomb's unveiling would be under-whelming due to the lack of danger in our journey. However, we were wrong. Very wrong. When we finally arrived at the cave and turned our flashlights to the walls, we were stunned. It was amazing. Still visible on the cave walls were paintings done centuries and centuries ago: Heracles' defeat of the Nemean Lion, Perseus's slaying of Medusa, Achilles' fall, and so many more. Unreal. And there in the center of the cave was a stone coffin. It had to be him.

It took all of our strength to push the lid off. Then the smell sent us reeling. A decayed human is bad enough, but a decayed half-human/half-horse. . . . We were finally able to bring ourselves back to the coffin. There in his skeletal hand was a large scroll. We played Rock, Paper, Scissors to see who'd reach in and grab it. Erika won. We unwound the scroll a little, careful not to rip the ancient papyrus, and then put our Ancient Greek translation skills to use. It was some sort of handbook—for heroes. Suddenly the whole cave rumbled. We took the scroll and fled.

Now, we're not idiots. We realize that cave paintings that old couldn't possibly remain that vibrant. And know a body and scroll from ancient times would be much more deteriorated. And that there's no such thing as centaurs . . . at least we *thought* we knew those things. The experience was too real to be faked and the scroll, which we've translated herein, too important to be dismissed. Someone—or something—wanted us to find the scroll and share it with the world. Though that proved to be an adventure in and of itself.

Since we're used to reading the Ancient Greek of Homer and Herodotus in cleaned, typed volumes accompanied by the grammar notes of an (often) helpful professor of Classics, the scroll was a challenge. Over the course of many sleepless nights, we struggled through the text of Chiron's instructions, fighting to find the best renderings of his colloquial (though still considerably epic) Greek into something that made sense in modern English. While we have took the care to be as accurate as possible in representing the grammar and phrasing of the original work, yet still retain a sense of Chiron's signature style, we confess that we have had to make some adaptations, and indeed, concessions, in formatting this book for a modern audience.

Over the course of translating this work, we feel that we have come to a deeper understanding of Greek heroes and the culture that surrounded them. We thought our own jobs were hard, constantly grading papers—but it's no battle against the hydra! We hope that reading Chiron's handbook will similarly inspire you on your own personal quest, whatever it may be.

ERIKA CARLSON + HEATHER DAY

ACKNOWLEDGMENTS

We would like to thank the many people who helped us in translating and preparing this work for the masses. Beginning with the students and teachers of the various departments which gave us the skills to decode Chiron's guide, including Bryn Mawr, Haverford, and Wheaton College, as well as the University of Maryland at College Park. We would also like to extend our gratitude to our respective parents for all of their support. Special thanks go out to our fellow classicists Aaron Hershkowitz and Ashish George for their help in translating the more difficult passages. But most of all we are extraordinarily grateful to the pantheon of the Greek Gods for accepting our various sacrifices and allowing us to share this work with other mortals.

WELCOME TO

CHIRON ENTERPRISES

CHAPTER 1

INTRO TO HEROISM

THE ANCIENT AND THE AWESOME

Sing, all ye Muses, the glorious deeds
Of the bronze-clad heroes, well-greaved, swift-footed,
Voluminous in luxuriant locks,
Those battlers of the monstrous hordes that scourged
The vast earth and the much-thundering depths.
Tell me, heavenly sisters nine, dancing with delicate white ankles,
Whose mighty teachings fostered them as fledglings,
Guided their green years, coaxed their characters
Into the condition commensurate with conquest?

And whose indeed? It is he,
He who dwelled among the peaks of Pelion,
He, the doubled in form, and also in wisdom,
Son of Cronus, father to the lost sons of Achaea,
The mentor to heroes—Chiron the centaur!

Thanks, Rhapsodes, for that heartfelt introduction. Pardon my interruption, but it seems we've gathered quite the crowd. Greetings, *hoi polloi*. I am none other than Chiron the Centaur, of Chiron Enterprises, here today to share what made the greats great. So pay attention and follow this guide to heroics if you want to join the ranks of Theseus, Heracles, and Oedipus. Well, not that last one—*that* weirdo wasn't one of my students. (But we'll cover some of the things he did right, even so.)

Anyway. Why do you want to become a hero? Maybe you're an altruist hooked on good deeds—like freeing damsels in distress, or liberating kingdoms from monsters with bad, sometimes even fiery, breath. Or maybe you're looking to journey to exotic foreign lands in search of mystical objects as souvenirs. . . . Or maybe you simply want to star in your own epic, and are in it for the glory alone. (No shame in that!) Whatever your motivation, this guide will get you there.

I'll help you get from point alpha to point omega on your chosen quest. And for nautical types who are lost without GPS—I'm looking at *you*, Odysseus—I'll get you back safe, even if it takes a decade. We'll go over the tools of the heroic trade, from the conventional sword-and-shield combo to using farm equipment when you're caught by surprise. Then I'll show you how to use those tools to slay monsters you might encounter while questing. Finally, because retirement has been the downfall of many a hero, I'll help you adjust to domestic life once you're ready to hang up your helmet and sword.

Is that laughter I hear from the audience? Well, I'm not talking out of my horse's ass, but I bet you're thinking, "Who does this half-beast think he is? What's *he* ever done?" Let me tell you a little about my role as a mentor to heroes—I've trained the best and observed the rest. And I've got the testimonials to prove it.

4

So let's take a look at Achaea's best heroes. Then *maybe* you'll be ready for a lesson or two in questing.

> Chiron Enterprises does not hold itself responsible for any accidents and/or incidents involving murderous wives, poisoned arrows, jealous kings standing on cliffs, falling pieces of ships, or raving Bacchantes.

⊰ HEROES TO WORSHIP ⊱

✦ HERACLES, SON OF ZEUS ✦

HOMETOWN: Thebes

CATCH PHRASE: "Let's go clubbing!"

CLAIM TO FAME: Heracles was an athlete from the cradle. His first sport? Extreme Serpent Strangling, which he took up at the tender age of two minutes when the goddess Hera sent snakes to disturb his nap. From there, he moved on to tackle bigger, meaner, and more poisonous animals, including clubbing the Nemean Lion, whose skin later became his preferred battle garb. From the Garden of the Hesperides to the Underworld to Mount Olympus, there's nowhere this hero hasn't left his mark.

5

Perseus, son of Zeus, proudly in possession of Medusa's head

✦ PERSEUS, ALSO SON OF ZEUS ✦

HOMETOWN: Argos

CATCH PHRASE: "Gotta do what you can to get a-*head* in life!"

CLAIM TO FAME: Feeling boxed in from life with Mom, Perseus eventually flew the nest to go a-questing. A pit stop with Medusa's neighbors, the Gray Sisters, helped him set his eye on chopping off the Gorgon Medusa's head, which had hair so bad even *it* recoiled.

✦ BELLEROPHON, SON OF GLAUCUS ✦

HOMETOWN: Corinth

CATCH PHRASE: "The only way to fly!"

CLAIM TO FAME: This brave hero went on several quests, ranging from battles against the Solymi men to the Amazonian women to most spectacularly a fire-breathing lion/snake/goat hybrid, known as the Chimaera. His slaying of this strange beast made him a legendary hero. And his flying horse, Pegasus, made him one of the few heroes who knew how to travel in style.

✦ THESEUS, SON OF AEGEUS AND POSEIDON ✦ (IT'S COMPLICATED)

HOMETOWN: Athens

CATCH PHRASE: "Grab life by the horns!"

CLAIM TO FAME: Despite his occasional tendency to forget minor details, such as his father or girlfriend, Theseus rose to daunting tasks such as driving outlaws from Attica's Old West and navigating the Cretan Labyrinth. No bull—if you're in the market for someone to slay the Minotaur, Theseus is your man.

→ ATALANTA, DAUGHTER OF SCHOINEUS OR IASOS ← (IT'S EVEN MORE COMPLICATED)

HOMETOWN: The Arcadian wilderness

CATCH PHRASE: "The key to heroism? Lead a *boar*ing life!"

CLAIM TO FAME: An agile runner, hunter, and wrestler, this heroine sure can play in the big leagues. An independent, albeit somewhat wild woman, Atalanta wrestled and hunted alongside the great heroes of her day. She was the first to draw blood from the monstrous porker that ravaged Calydon. She even killed some of my cousins, but that's fine with me, they were bullies anyway.

→ JASON, SON OF AESON ←

HOMETOWN: Iolchus

CATCH PHRASE: "Row, row, row my boat."

CLAIM TO FAME: A Boy Scout from the time he helped the disguised goddess Hera across the river, Jason knew that the best way to achieve anything was to be prepared. He also understood that it's important your friends have your back. As master and commander of the *Argo*, Jason assembled the eclectic talents of many a hero and the occasional hot chick to aid him in bringing back the Golden Fleece.

→ORPHEUS, SON OF APOLLO←

HOMETOWN: Thrace

CATCH PHRASE: "Never look back!"

CLAIM TO FAME: Even the rocks rock out to his tunes. In a battle of the bands, Orpheus's riffs were so intense that his opponents, the Sirens themselves, forgot their lyrics. After his tour with the Argonauts, he gave a special, one-night-only performance in the Underworld, where reports held that even the Lord of the Dead swooned. Unfortunately, a quick glance back at his wife before the tour was over cost him the chance at a reunion duet.

→OEDIPUS, SON OF LAIUS←

HOMETOWN: Thebes; no, wait: Corinth; no, wait: Thebes

CATCH PHRASE: "For a private eye, it's always an open-and-shut case."

CLAIM TO FAME: This brilliant detective solved several cases while going a-questing. He first came onto the scene after ridding Thebes of the riddling Sphinx, a creature with an appetite for answers or your friend Alexander. Having conquered the beast, Oedipus inherited the kingdom and a hot wife—more on that awkward honeymoon later. Another case crossed his path years later, when Oedipus inspected the scene of a murdered king, eventually solving the crime through some useful background checks. There are no crimes in all of Boeotia that this hero couldn't solve.

9

✦ ACHILLES, SON OF PELEUS ✦

HOMETOWN: Phthia (try saying that one without spitting)

CATCH PHRASE: "Time wounds all heels."

CLAIM TO FAME: Swift-footed and mad about glory, Achilles can truly be called the best of the Achaeans—annihilator of Amazon queens, truncator of the Trojan hordes, death-dealer to the dwellers of the Dardanelles Mountains. But, well, let's face it, he moped a lot. We all have our bad days though, and if Achilles was an expert at anything, it was at how to turn a bad day for your love life into a good day on the battlefield.

✦ ODYSSEUS, SON OF LAERTES ✦

HOMETOWN: Ithaca

CATCH PHRASE: "Cleverness will keep you afloat!"

CLAIM TO FAME: Those of you who favor brains over brawn might find inspiration in this island-hopper. After a successful career devising tactics for the Greeks during the Trojan War—and winning a special commendation for his Equine Strategy—he hit all of the fantastic tourist attractions on the way back, from the home of the Cyclops to Circe's island.

✦ AENEAS, SON OF ANCHISES ✦

HOMETOWN: Troy

CATCH PHRASE: "It's not you, it's my quest."

CLAIM TO FAME: This pious man redefines the heroic mold, as he ran from the danger of his burning city, to rescue his aging father and his young son. This poor victim of Hera's rage was sent from coast to coast as well as to the Underworld looking for a new home for his people. This family man became the founding hero of a small town called Rome.

Lesson Learned

As you can see from this assortment of tales, not only is heroism a diverse and growing field, but it's also a lucrative one. To emulate the strength of Heracles, the cunning of Odysseus, or the self-righteous mortal angst of Achilles, you'll need to listen up, sharpen your spear, and get ready for adventure!

KEEP THE GODS CLOSE . . .

AND YOUR FAMILY CLOSER

WHO'S YOUR DADDY?

MAKING THE BEST OF NEPOTISM

Parents can be obnoxious. However, they play a big role in the person you are and the type of hero you will become. Their nagging to take out the trash and drive the cattle out to the field may be annoying, but your parents are more crucial now than they were before. Accept it and move on.

For one thing, they need to teach you about your family history. On the battlefield, you must recite at least three generations of ancestry along with highlights from your family's past before engaging your enemy in combat. So listen closely to Mom and Dad, memorize your lineage, and brush up on anecdotes about your relatives—preferably the kind in which your father slew a fire-breathing winged leopard, not the kind where your drunk uncle puked all over your grandmother at the last Panathenaea Festival. Stories of valor work best . . . no matter how amusing the embarrassing ones are. Be ready to rattle all this off at the drop of a helmet. An inarticulate hero is a dead hero.

15

⚛ THE SON OF A GOD ⚛

THE PRODUCT OF IMMORTALITY
AND INFIDELITY

Having trouble with your combat entrance? If your mom and dad leave something to be desired, there may be an underlying divine reason. Are your physical features nothing like theirs? Do they lack any semblance of an adventurous spirit, babbling on about boring land taxes while you plan your epic quests? Does every family quarrel end with you shouting "That's it—I must be adopted!"? Well, you may be on to something. There's a good chance that the mom or dad who nags you to fetch water at the *agora* isn't even your parent. Lucky you! One of them probably got it on with a god, and you're a special delivery from Mount Olympus.

A Battefield Welcome

HERE'S AN EXAMPLE OF A PROPER BATTLEFIELD WELCOME FROM THE TROJAN WARRIOR GLACUS: "I am from a beautiful city in the heart of Argos, called Ephyra, where Sisyphus once roamed. This Sisyphus had a son named Glaucus, who was father to Bellerophon, who slew the mighty Chimaera from atop the winged horse Pegasus. This hero fathered the great Hippolokhos, mine own sire."

Much better than saying, "My dad's name is Nikias, and he called his pop Agathon."

Statistically speaking, your mom most likely hooked up with Zeus, the lightning-slinging king of the gods. (His allure is hard for the ladies to resist.) Still, you could also be the offspring of the sea-god Poseidon, the beautiful Aphrodite, or another powerful deity. Just about any mortal-immortal matchup will work to your advantage.

Why's that? Let's go over the perks of a divine lineage.

PERK #1: You're now half god, which means you're prettier, faster, stronger, and smarter (well, usually).

PERK #2: There are material benefits. Prepare to receive some really sweet birthday gifts. Mom or Dad probably put in a special order for your eighteenth with the blacksmith god Hephaestus, whose shields, swords, and spears are the stuff of legend. Your enemies will be shaking in their sandals when they see you wielding one of his brightly burnished handicrafts.

PERK #3: You're harder to kill. When your lifestyle involves facing off against fire-breathing, snake-tailed monstrosities and surviving shipwrecks, you'll be grateful for this perk.

So there are some big benefits to having a parent who just can't say no to a god.

⚜ CROWNING YOUR CAP ⚜
DISCOVERING YOUR ROYAL STYLE

Don't lose hope if you're not the offspring of some Olympian. Your parents still might not be your real parents. You may be

King of Heavenly Hookups

Zeus has a way with the ladies. Here are some of his more notorious conquests:

IO: The king of the gods' secret lover; their trysts occurred under a cover of clouds, until Hera grew suspicious of the overcast skies. Zeus turned Io into a cow.

ALCMENE: Zeus decided to seduce this happily married queen of Thebes by taking the form of her husband. Needless to say, it was quite a surprise when the king came home early.

EUROPA: Zeus cut through the bull with this one . . . by taking the form of a bull. Charging away with her to Crete, their union created the bloodline that would eventually produce the Minotaur.

DANAE: Even being locked away by her dad couldn't keep Zeus at bay. He took the form of a golden shower, rained upon the princess, and left a sparkle in their son Perseus's eyes.

LEDA: If Zeus's method of attraction wasn't weird enough— taking the form of a swan—the princess gave birth to two sets of twins hatched from two different eggs.

a misplaced child of royal blood. It doesn't matter how you ended up that way—whether you were placed in a box or left behind on a mountain—you are still a member of the royal family. Your actual family may even greet you with open arms, provided you aren't fated to kill them, as sometimes happens. Consult an oracle before locating your birth parents, just in case. If it turns out the welcome party won't be that welcoming, disguise yourself and sneak into the palace before claiming your birthright.

✦ RECOGNITION TOKENS:
YOUR PRINCELY PASSWORD ✦

The monarchy doesn't usually welcome outsiders. Otherwise, any average Dikaiopolis could lay claim to the crown. So before you show up on Mom and Dad's royal doorstep, you need to locate your recognition token. This item was left behind in your infancy and proves your legitimacy as an heir. Basically, it's your membership card to the Clubs Royale of Greece. Search everywhere. Leave no rock unturned. After all, Theseus became heir to the Athenian throne once he discovered his father's old weapons under a boulder. Imagine what might be hidden in your backyard!

Chiron Enterprises takes no responsibility for any legal consequences or parental groundings that result from search-related property damage. Digging up your mother's prize garden is not advised.

→WHEN SCARRED FOR LIFE IS A GOOD THING←

For those of you who dug up the garden only to destroy the local vineyard, you may want to look at yourself instead. No, I'm not suggesting you open a vein to check for blue blood. Rather, inspect your body for old scars; they're very revealing. Odysseus, for instance, bore a hunting scar on his thigh that allowed him to be recognized after twenty years away from home. On the other hand, if you have scars like Oedipus on your ankles, watch out. It's likely someone wanted you dead. A nail through the feet is said to keep ghosts from walking. There's a good chance that King Dad left you on the side of the road as a baby, hoping you'd never come back.

Lesson Learned

Family matters. Whether you come from a long line of heroes, a messy monarchy, or by way of Mount Olympus, your roots will keep you grounded during your quest. When things get out of hand, it's always important to know who in your family has your back—or is waiting to stab you in it.

CHAPTER
3

MAD MONARCHY

DERANGED DYNASTIES
YOU *DON'T WANT* TO JOIN

I t's great to suddenly find out you're the long-lost son or daughter of a king, but in a few rare instances, you may wish you'd stayed with your adopted peasant parents—no matter how lame it was to herd sheep all day. There, your brothers and sisters beat you up and took your snacks. Here, they'll try to murder you and take your throne.

Of course, occasionally a hero is born into one of these crown-wearing clans, and manages to gain a certain amount of glory anyway. But remember, you have just as much chance of ending up dead when you hang out with these sorts of folks (and they can get very creative about it, too). So, while you still might wind up as the subject of verses of epic poetry, it may be for all the wrong reasons. Are you willing to take those risks?

⁂ ROYAL FAMILY REUNION? ⁂
(I THINK I'LL PASS.)

Sure, a herald could arrive any day inviting you to rejoin
your lost parents or siblings in their palatial home, but how do
you know they're not going to be murderous crazies? That's
easy—pay attention to the patronymic. For your benefit, your
buddy Chiron will list the names of the most dysfunctional
heroic families here, so you know which invitations to decline.
Or, you can show up for one of the family barbecues—but
make sure you've got a dagger up your sleeve for self-defense,
and a side dish of your own making! Because you never know
who's going to attempt to kill you, and if someone's prepared
an entrée of human flesh, you'll want something else to snack
on. (It never hurts to be prepared.)

Chiron Enterprises takes no responsibility for bizarre
revenge attempts and any subsequent, and ironically
backfiring, aftermath inspired by these family histories.
Such narratives should be taken as words of caution
rather than as models for proper behavior. Do not
try cannibalism or parricide at home. In addition, all
exposures and exiles of ill-destined firstborn sons should
be carried out by professionals rather than amateurs.

→ PROCNE, PHILOMELA, AND KING TEREUS OF THRACE ←

FAMILY MOTTO: "There's nothing that can't be resolved through a nice family dinner!"

BLACK SHEEP: We suspect that Itys, the youngest family member, may have been one, but of course he never lived long enough for us to find out.

There is no shortage of crappy husbands in ancient Greece, but Tereus's treatment of his wife, Procne, and the subsequent fallout, lands him in the top five. The story goes like this: He'd much rather have married Procne's sister, Philomela, so he tried to start up a little somethin' on the side. Philomela rejected him outright, so Tereus cut out her tongue to keep his secret safe.

But Tereus didn't count on the fact that Procne and Philomela had their own secret code. Philomela wove a message to Procne in a piece of cloth, letting her know the deal. Working together, the sisters plotted their revenge. They decided what he needed was a nice, home-cooked meal—made from the flesh of his own son, Itys. Imagine the indigestion it caused him when he found *that* out.

For some reason, the only punishment the gods could dole out for this dysfunctional family was to turn them into birds. Usually, the gods are much more creative than that; guess they were feeling generous that day. Anyway, you now know Procne and Philomela as nightingales and Tereus as the hoopoe. Next time someone remarks on how beautifully they sing, let them know the song is probably about maiming, cannibalism, and murder.

→THE ROYAL HOUSES OF THEBES←

MOTTO: "When we say coat of arms, we're talking swords, spears, and anything pointy."

BLACK SHEEP: Ismene, the youngest daughter, who wishes everyone would just shut up and stop quarreling for once.

It's the ultimate oxymoron: A goddess named Harmonia causes total discord among her family members. When Harmonia married Cadmus, founder of the city of Thebes, she received a necklace that caused generations of grief and aggravation. Worst wedding gift ever . . . at least until Eris dropped the Apple of Discord at the wedding of Peleus and Thetis. But that's another story.

Some of the worst effects of the necklace's curse surfaced with Cadmus's grandsons, Actaeon and Pentheus.

PENTHEUS VS. DIONYSUS

Pentheus, Cadmus's uptight and overly moral grandson, denied the divinity of his cousin Dionysus and tried to prevent his groupies—the Maenads—from having any fun outside the city limits. Forget letting your hair down during his reign! Bad move on Pentheus's part. Before you knew it, Dionysus, god of madness and wine, had him wearing a dress, climbing a tree, and being torn to pieces by his own mother and aunts.

MORAL OF THE STORY: Don't tear yourself apart trying to keep your life in order (the gods'll do that for you!).

24

Pentheus, after Dionysus
loosened him up

ACTAEON VS. ARTEMIS

While out strolling through the woods with his faithful hounds, Actaeon accidentally caught Artemis bathing in the woods. Instead of going easy on the poor guy, Artemis turned him into a stag and rendered him defenseless. Actaeon's dogs were unable to find their master, but soon took comfort in the fact that they were eating their favorite dinner that night—raw venison.

MORAL OF THE STORY: Sometimes, it's best to leap before you look.

LAIUS VS. CHRYSIPPUS

Later on down the road, a man called Laius became the king of Thebes. Laius was of an entirely different bloodline, but seemed to pick up Theban bad habits from the soil itself. He also had a strange idea of what was constitutes a good time. During the reckless days of his youth, Laius kidnapped a young prince named Chrysippus from a neighboring kingdom. The prince died during the abduction, and his father cursed Laius and his descendants, bringing yet another round of fun to the Theban royals. Laius and his wife Jocasta's first and only kid was a son named Oedipus, who oracles claimed would kill his father and marry his mother. . . .

MORAL OF THE STORY: What goes around comes around (and around, and around). . . .

ETEOCLES VS. POLYNICES

It started with the sibling rivalry between Oedipus's kids, Eteocles and Polynices. Their disagreement as to who would rule Thebes in their father's absence came to a head in a bloody battle that tore the city apart, and left both brothers dead.

Their uncle Creon was left to pick up the pieces, and since Polynices had been the one to invade the city, Creon declared him a traitor and left his body unburied as punishment. Without a proper funeral, Polynices's soul couldn't make a proper passage to the underworld. (Charon, the ferryman of the dead, is picky about dead souls having exact fares.)

MORAL OF THE STORY: When it's political power, sharing is never caring.

ANTIGONE VS. CREON

What Creon didn't count on was Antigone, Oedipus's daughter, who'd inherited her father's stubborn attitude. Antigone decided Polynices would be buried no matter what, even if she had to do it twice. Creon's answer was to ground Antigone—literally—in a cave where she'd be buried alive. But he changed his mind and re-opened the cave, only to find that Antigone had already hanged herself in her veil (maybe it seemed better than starving to death?). In a quick chain reaction of suicides, Creon's son Haman—who'd been engaged to marry Antigone—fell on his own sword, and then Creon's wife, Eurydice, killed herself out of grief over her son's death. All in all, not Creon's best day.

MORAL OF THE STORY: Death can be catchy. Honestly, those Thebans. You think they would have learned by now.

27

✦ THE HOUSE OF ATREUS ✦

FAMILY MOTTO: Revenge is a dish best served cold. Also hot. And as lukewarm leftovers. And always with a side of your opponents' children.

BLACK SHEEP: Menelaus, who despite having a wife who caused a war, didn't rival his relatives in the murderous insanity department.

The family history of the Atreids is so complicated you'd need a flow chart to get it; what's more, that chart would flow with the blood of doomed family members. Situated in Mycenae, the Atreids were a brutal and competitive bunch; they worked hard to outdo each other with generation after generation of heinous crimes.

GENERATION ALPHA:
THE HOST WITH THE MOST . . . AUDACITY, THAT IS

It started with Tantalus, the patriarch of this murderous clan, who'd invited the gods over for a feast. Looking for a dish to whet their appetites, he thought his son Pelops might do just perfectly if cooked with the right seasonings. Pelops, it turns out, didn't agree with the menu. As punishment, the gods sentenced Tantalus to eternal food torture in the Underworld. Or rather, lack-of-food torture. Tantalus sat beneath a tree full of grapes and in front of a pool full of water. When he tried to drink, the waters would recede. When he tried to pluck grapes for a snack, the tree branch jumped out of his reach.

GENERATION BETA:
EXTREME SPORTS, EXTREME CHEATING

On to the next generation: Pelops's childhood stint as an entrée for the immortals didn't exactly make him the most stable adult. Once he was pieced back together and fitted with a cool ivory shoulder to replace the one Demeter ate, he grew up, got married, and started the next generation of murders. He set his sights on Hippodameia, the extremely beautiful daughter of Oenomaus—an uber-protective dad. Oenomaus said no man could have his daughter unless he beat him in a chariot race. Pelops accepted the challenge and promptly worked out a way to cheat. He found an ally in Myrtilus, Oenomaus's charioteer, who replaced the bronze axles of his master's chariot with soft beeswax. It caused quite a traffic pileup! And since sabotage wasn't enough for this badass, Pelops drowned Myrtilus soon after.

GENERATION GAMMA:
CHIPS OFF THE OLD EXECUTIONER'S BLOCK

Atreus and Thyestes, Pelops's kids, took after their dad. Thyestes ran off with things very dear to Atreus—his wife and the golden ram that secured his right to rule the kingdom. Atreus, in turn, began plotting his revenge. Recalling his grandfather's diabolical dinner, he cooked up a stew for Thyestes . . . made from Thyestes' two sons.

GENERATION DELTA:
OUT OF THE COOKING POT AND ONTO
THE SACRIFICIAL ALTAR

For a while, it looked as if Atreus's own sons, Agamemnon and Menelaus, had escaped the drama of past generations. But then the in-laws decided to get in on the nasty family business. Menelaus's wife Helen eloped with the Trojan prince Paris (we'll get those details later) kicking off a ten-year war. But they could only get the wind to sail to Troy if Agamemnon sacrificed his daughter Iphigenia with a knife to the throat. When they returned home, Agamemnon was murdered by his wife Clytemnestra (Helen's sister, by the way) and his cousin Aegisthus, whom she had taken as a new lover.

GENERATION EPSILON:
END OF THE LINE?

It should have ended there, but Clytemnestra and Agamemnon's surviving kids came by their murderous ways honestly. Orestes, their son, returned from the exile he'd been forced into as a child, collected his melodramatic sister Electra, and together they killed off both their mother and Aegisthus. Well, more or less together. Orestes stabbed them, while Electra helped to hold the sword and jumped up and down in manic glee.

Killing a family member means the Furies are going to be all over you—and Electra and Orestes were no exception. They ran all the way to Athens, where they were judged for the murder of their mother. Things got so crazy that the gods finally had to step in to get the House of Atreus to chill out.

There were so few Atreids left at that point, it might have actually worked.

As you can see, having royal relations can cement your reputation as a hero and allow you to inherit a kingdom. But if you join a dysfunctional family like these, you'll also become famous because of wacky genealogies. Note that the first option is not without its drawbacks. No matter how warmly Mom and Dad welcome you back to the palace, there will *always* be some cranky next-of-kin claiming you cut in line for the throne. They may even take measures to get rid of you once and for all, in which case you're going to have to find clever ways of staying alive. More on that in the following section.

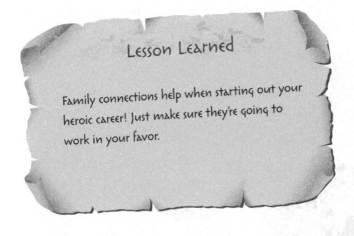

Lesson Learned

Family connections help when starting out your heroic career! Just make sure they're going to work in your favor.

31

CHAPTER 4

RECLAIMING THE "FUN" IN DYS*FUNC*TIONAL

THANK GOD FOR GODS

Let's say your disgruntled uncle has sent you off on a seemingly doomed errand to get some unattainable item. What do you do? Well, don't panic. Your uncle has already proven he's a wimp by not killing you on his own. And, he's just set you up for something that'll give you good publicity—a heroic quest. While you're busy impressing the populace of your kingdom by slaying monsters, your rival for the crown will be cowering in fear from any creature you bring back as a souvenir.

⊰ QUESTING ⊱

AT THE BEHEST OF EVIL RELATIVES

Taking the heroic high ground is infinitely helpful in dealing with mortal nuisances, but things get trickier if you're related to the gods. Remember that stat about the number of heroes that

33

are sons of Zeus? Here's another: 100 percent of those heroes are pushed around by Zeus's jealous wife, Hera. In fact, Hera's such a bully she even creates problems for heroes who aren't related to Zeus! Just ask Aphrodite's son Aeneas.

To be fair, rumor has it that Aeneas's descendents are fated to eventually destroy Hera's favorite city, but the fact that she plans ahead for something that hasn't even happened yet just goes to show how touchy Hera can be. Any misstep can provoke divine wrath, so learn the dos and don'ts of messing with the deities *before* you head out on your quest.

BAD IDEA: KILLING, MAIMING, OR OTHERWISE INCAPACITATING GODS' KIDS

Odysseus left the Cyclops blind and angry, not realizing that the one-eyed giant was Poseidon's son. After that, the hero faced unusually rough seas in his futile attempts to get back to Ithaca.

BAD IDEA: POACHING THE HIGHER POWERS' PETS

Mycenaean high king Agamemnon killed a deer belonging to the hunting goddess, Artemis. Forget about a simple fine for poaching. In order to sail to Troy, Artemis required Agamemnon to kill his own daughter, Iphigenia, as payment for offing her prized pet.

BAD IDEA: TRESPASSING ON THE DIVINE'S PRIVATE PROPERTY

Stay away from their pets and definitely stay out of their yards. Greek hero Philoctetes learned this the hard way.

On his way to Troy, Philoctetes wandered into a divine wood and received the nastiest wound ever recorded in the healing god Asclepius's medical files. A good rule of thumb is to steer clear of the gods' stuff.

GOOD IDEA: HELPING LITTLE OLD LADIES CROSS THE RIVER

It may sound trite (and could cost you a sandal), but practice proper etiquette when it comes to the elderly because you never know who could be hiding behind a wrinkly disguise. Take it from Jason, who was psyched to learn the old woman he helped across a river was really Hera. His good manners scored him support from the queen of the gods for his entire quest.

With the tempers of both the mortals and the immortals against you, you may think that farming sounds like a pretty good career right about now. But don't ditch the hero idea so quickly—help is on the way.

❧ ATHENA IS MY CO-CHARIOTEER ❧

So, we know the gods can be irritable and unpredictable, and this can become a problem if you aren't careful. But—lucky you!—the gods are also extremely prone to infighting. For any god who holds a vendetta against you for smashing his favorite temple, there's a rival god who's willing to take your side just to spite the other guy. The chart that follows gives the rundown of tempestuous relationships on Mount Olympus.

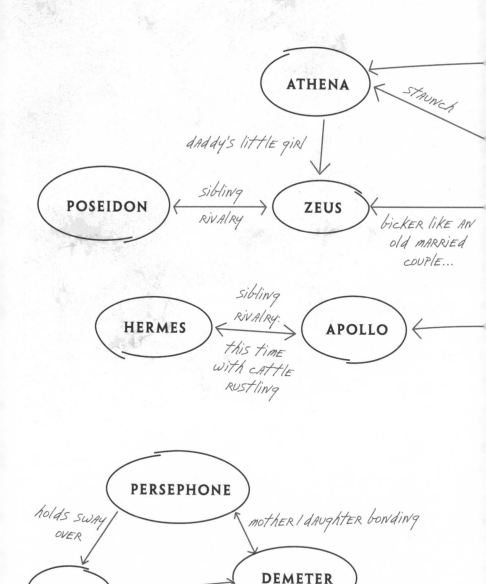

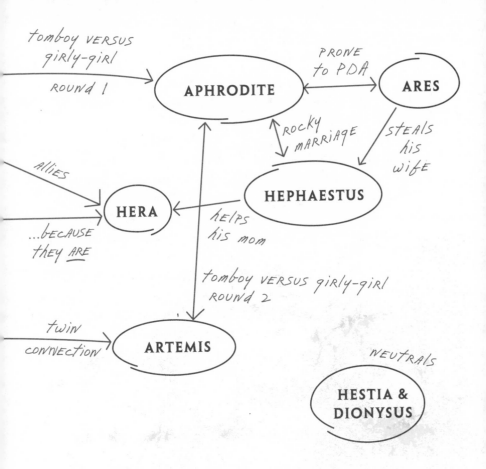

THE COMPLEX
RELATIONSHIPS
OF OLYMPUS

→ONE GOD'S NEMESIS
IS ANOTHER GOD'S DARLING←

Keep in mind that opposites do *not* always attract. Often your enemy god will enjoy hobbies that a potential divine sponsor finds either boring or hateful. So if Aphrodite's singled you out for some torment, pray to sportier virgin goddesses, like Artemis and Athena. Hermes, the trickster god, has been picking on his more serious brother Apollo since birth. So if the overworked musician-archer-prophet god doesn't take a shine to you, Hermes will surely help you out. That said, note that relationships between gods are volatile and subject to change at a moment's notice. You never know when Zeus and Hera's marriage counseling will finally start to take effect (though it could very well be the next Golden Age). . . .

If you'd rather not navigate the stormy family politics of Olympus, there are other ways to summon divine intervention. Sometimes, it's as easy as being in the right place at the right time. Gods tend to favor cities just as you or I might favor

Clash of the Olympians: Athena vs. Poseidon

How did Athena gain control over Athens? She won it through a contest. Each god provided a gift that they thought would be most useful to the city—Poseidon gave a salt spring and Athena gave an olive tree. The citizens of Athens and their king, Cecrops, voted on which they liked best. In the end, Athena's multifunctional olive tree won out—providing wood, oil for lamps, food, and other resources. Since then, Athena has been the official guardian of the city.

a chariot team. (Go Pelion Greens!) For instance, if you're from Athens, you've got instant support from Athena, who won control of the city from Poseidon practically at the beginning of time.

Obviously, there are perks to having a god on your side. We've already mentioned the cool armor you can score through your Hephaestus connection. Worried about keeping up appearances—and disappearances—on your quest? The gods can provide fabulous makeovers for when you need to stand out in a crowd, and convenient mists and disguises for when you're better off sneaking out the back. They can also hook you up with special transportation, whether Athena offers to be your designated driver (as she did for Diomedes during the Trojan War), or a deity provides you with a ship that talks (like the sweet ride Jason received from the goddess of wisdom).

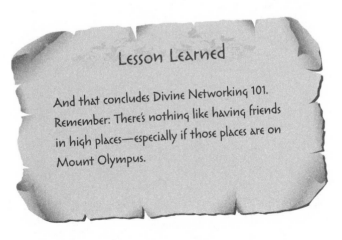

Lesson Learned

And that concludes Divine Networking 101. Remember: There's nothing like having friends in high places—especially if those places are on Mount Olympus.

DUDE, WHERE'S MY TRIREME?

THE HERO'S WAY

THE WHO, WHAT, WHERE OF QUESTING

So, you've finally done it. You've left the house—or been kicked out, depending. (Once you tell your parents you're actually the child of a god, they'll probably deny ever knowing you.) But now that you've hit the road in search of monsters to slay, there's just one question: Where are you going?

⊰ MAP YOUR QUEST ⊱

First, we'll tackle the cardinal directions, using Grecian city-states as our center.

NORTH

Here you'll find the Gray Sisters, who share one eye and one tooth. Somehow, the swapping of spit that goes along with this doesn't seem to faze them. But they also pass that eye and tooth back and forth, so you can't afford to be squeamish. Figure out how to get their attention—grabbing them in their eyeball is a good start—and they'll spill priceless information for your journey ahead. Just be quick about it. Perseus already used this trick, so the Gray Sisters will be on guard.

EAST

Look at where the sun rises every morning. As home to Persians and Trojans, the East is largely civilized and heavily perfumed, though its inhabitants still cling to the unmanly habit of wearing pants. It'll be up to you to show them that real men wear skirts.

SOUTH

In the South you'll find Ethiopians, a race with a culture so rich it seems legendary. While few young heroes have paid them a visit, their kingdom is a popular vacation spot for the gods. Whenever the gods aren't answering mortals' prayers, it's usually because they're too busy partying it up at the Ethiopians' fabulous barbecues. Keep this in mind—if you want to avoid running into a god when he's angry with you, don't travel south when they're en route to Ethiopia. If there's anything a god dislikes more than having their life disrupted because of you, it's having their lives disrupted when they're on vacation.

WEST

To the far West, where the sun sets, life also slips over the horizon. Here you'll discover the Underworld and other worlds populated by the long—and often not so long—deceased. Don't freak out at the idea of sailing off toward the horizon—

44

this is where you'll find some of your most exciting adventures! What's more, the dead are often a reliable source of information for your future, and you may get a chance to see long-lost pets or relatives.

Hopefully by now you've picked a path, because it's time to check out some other aspects of geography. Since an endless variety of beasts are yours for the slaying, you'll want to narrow your options by choosing your preferred terrain. You know your strengths and weaknesses best, so keep them in mind as you consider what part of the world makes for your ideal questing spot. That way, you won't be caught chasing a monster up mountains with only your beach sandals, because you'll have packed footwear for hiking. If you're working toward a reputation as a well-rounded hero, you'll want to pay extra attention to geography. Remember, different locations host different kinds of monsters. Knowing what lives where will keep you prepared as you embark on your journey.

That said, let's break the wide world of heroism down into three broad categories—the land, the water, and the ever-popular realms of the dead.

⊰ THE LAND ⊱

For many young heroes, this location feels like the closest to home, so land adventures sound boring. Take a closer look, though, and you'll realize that the land can be uber-diverse. And the farther you go from Greece, the less things are going to seem like your childhood farm. Monsters lurk in the depths of a dark forest, hide in the peaks of a mountain, or burrow at the base of a volcano. Proceed with extreme caution in any of these areas! Each is full of its own special sorts of threats.

✦ MOUNTAINS ✦

It's easy enough to die falling from a cliff when pushed by your opponent or a jealous friend. But accidents happen, too, so watch your step—and your back. For extra safety, bring magical objects that allow you to take flight, in the off chance that you find yourself hurtling toward Earth. Another tip: Make friends with winged creatures like Pegasus (but avoid winged gods such as Eros, who, as Aphrodite's son, takes great delight in making people fall in love with the wrong person).

MOUNTAIN GEAR CHECKLIST

- ☐ Hiking sandals (preferably with wings)
- ☐ Cloak for colder climates
- ☐ Ambrosia-supplemented cake for an energy boost

✦ VOLCANOES ✦

Volcanic areas are a natural home to fire-breathing creatures. Once again, try to pack some magical items for protection; this time, you'll want fireproof ointments. See your local witch for help, but make sure she doesn't screw you on price. These fireproof ointments should protect you from the sun, and the scorching breath of monsters, leaving you with a nice, even tan as opposed to a peeling and painful sunburn. This tan is a testament to your time spent in the great outdoors, a true mark of your heroic status.

It's Not You, It's the Hunting: Artemis's Posse and the Story of Callisto

Artemis isn't the only girl ever to forgo a relationship for her career. Even aside from her companionship with other goddesses like Athena and Hestia who are more focused on war and homemaking, respectively, Artemis has a crowd of nymphs who are following in her footsteps. They may be gorgeous, and you may want to invite them out on a hunting date, but you may as well forget it. Since these beauties are often found hunting by Artemis's side, it's difficult to get any alone time with them. As you may have learned from approaching them on festival days, there's nothing more intimidating than a whole cluster of girls. What's more, they probably just won't like you very much.

In fact, courting one of Artemis's nymphs is such a stupid idea that only Zeus can get away with it—and that's because *never* doesn't apply to the king of the gods. At one point, Zeus developed a crush on Artemis's companion Callisto. Deciding it would be best to win her over as a friend first, he took on the form of Artemis herself. When Zeus started getting too chummy, Artemis walked in on the couple. She turned Callisto into a bear for her transgression, but Zeus got away without punishment. He's an exception to the rule. In your case, Artemis wouldn't be as merciful.

47

VOLCANIC GEAR CHECKLIST

☐ Fireproof ointment

☐ Extra water to drink

☐ Even more water to put out fires

☐ Extra-thick soled sandals

→ THE FOREST ←

You may think you're used to the forest's wild animals after years of hunting with Dad, but this is one place where the *girls* are actually scarier than the monsters! After all, the forest is the domain of the goddess Artemis. Take it from Actaeon (the hero who was ripped apart by his own hunting dogs), you don't want to walk in on her in the bath.

Don't try to chat up any of Artemis's nymph companions, either. As pretty as they are and as much as you'd like them along to keep a lonely hero company, the goddess of the hunt won't have it. What's more, she'll probably punish the nymph as much as she punishes you, so you'll get the object of your newfound affection into a lot of trouble.

FOREST GEAR CHECKLIST

☐ Spear

☐ Bows and Arrows

☐ Best sandals for walking quietly

☐ Bright hunting cloak, so no one shoots you by accident

☐ Your trustiest hunting hounds

✦ LAND MONSTERS ✦

OK, so let's return to our menagerie of beastly creatures out there for the slaying. Fighting off land monsters is like a hunting trip gone extreme. While a land monster might resemble something familiar to you, it's usually a bigger and tougher version of it.

Calydonian Boar

Take the Calydonian Boar, for instance. It was so massive that it made regular boars look like nursing piglets.

For more information on battling the boar, see page 76.

Nemean Lion

Likewise, if you thought everyday lions were bad, wait until you encounter one with impenetrable skin! Heracles met such a lion in Nemea, and, after strangling it, he had to skin it with its own claws in order to turn its hide into his trademark fashion statement. On the other hand, land monsters are so big, their pelts and hides make great trophies, and conveniently function as clothing.

For more information on fighting this fierce beast, see page 74.

Giants

You're not out of the woods yet. You may also meet human-shaped monsters on your journey. Some can spring up out of nowhere—or from the ground itself, like the earth-born

49

warriors Jason defeated in Colchis. For others, think bigger and tougher, more GIANT. These vertically gifted troublemakers are standard fare for a young hero just starting out. You probably think you've got the smarts and agility to defeat a Giant. And you're probably right.

However, take this helpful pointer from your wise old friend Chiron: The name *Giant* means "Child of the Earth," which means that they derive strength from the ground beneath them. To take on a Giant, make sure you first have a way of getting it up (so to speak). Take a page from Heracles' playbook: He defeated the Giant Antaeus by lifting him off the ground! The Daedalan minds out there may be able to work a complex pulley system. The key is to get the Giant onto the platform without him noticing, so you'll need to work out the appropriate bait.

For more information on dealing with these oversize oafs, see page 100.

Snakes

You're keeping an eye peeled for oversized people and game, but you should also keep an ear out—for hissing noises. Snakes (not puppies) are Mother Earth's prized pets, so they tend to be *everywhere*. I don't even mean crawling-around-on-the-ground everywhere; I mean snakes show up where they have no business being, like as the limbs of a monster. Snakes come in the many- headed, extra-large, and fire-breathing varieties.

In short: Be prepared for anything, and conquer your fear of snakes ahead of time. On the flip side, if you find the sight of a being with snake legs amusing, don't laugh so hard you let your guard down. It might look like those legs are useless, but these venomous fangs can still bite and paralyze. (You're just flat-out naïve if you think these beasts have harmless garden snakes as tails.)

There's no more information left on snakes . . . just watch your step!

Slaying land monsters is generally a good start for a hero on his first quest. But maybe you're sick of being a landlubber. Maybe you feel the call of the open seas, and the adventure that goes with it. If so, sail toward all the creatures you can find in . . .

⊰ THE WATER ⊱

Ocean travel is a lot harder than you might think. There's no traffic, but the sea is still home to a number of nautical hazards. You know about storms and pirates, but what about the Sympleglades, known to the locals simply as "the Clashing Rocks"? These craggy formations often disrupt trade with their tendency to crush anything that comes between them. What about Scylla the sea monster, who alongside Charybdis the whirlpool doesn't leave much room for your ship? No questing hero wants to be stuck between these two. (You've got to see it to believe how bad it is.) But don't panic and start rowing backward—navigating the waterworks is a true test of heroism.

Traversing the deeps offers other obstacles. What about an entire chorus of Sirens calling your name? Dealing with these ladies presents a challenge, especially for the hero with an oversize ego. One minute they'll enchant with a lovely little ballad about your eternal fame, and the next they'll persuade you to jump ship, and your blood will become tonight's fine wine for some big "fish."

✦ OCEAN GODS: WHEN WATER THROUGH YOUR FINGERS GIVES GOOD ADVICE ✦

With so many obstacles clogging up the seas, it's a wonder ships get anywhere at all. Sea monsters lurk everywhere, and one of the remarkable qualities of many ocean-dwelling creatures is their ability to shape-shift. Fluid like the water itself, these creatures don't hold one form for long. To control a slippery shape-shifter, be stubborn! Get a tight grip on the creature, and *keep on holding*. It may change forms a number of times as it attempts to escape your grasp, morphing into various animals and even elements of nature, such as a raging fire. However, the creature will eventually give up and revert to its original form, at which point you can slay it with ease (if it's not on your side). If it doesn't seem to have a problem with you, it's much more likely to give useful advice. Value any knowledge imparted by a shape-shifter—Proteus, the Old Man in the Sea, offers everything from travel directions to pointers on beekeeping! Why Proteus would need apiary expertise in the first place is anyone's guess, but you can't deny the novelty of such info, and it provides a hobby for when you need a break from heroics.

→ KEEPING ALERT ON SMALLER SHORES ←

Don't be surprised to encounter shape-shifters and creatures akin to sea monsters in smaller bodies of water, such as lakes, rivers, and springs. Remember: They may be smaller but the same dangers apply. Use similar tactics to fight them. Just because you're traveling through the woods along a stream doesn't mean you won't be fodder for form-changing nuisances.

> Chiron Enterprises takes no responsibility for any lost supplies, crew members, or senses of direction during one's journeys around the world. Directions should always be held firmly in one's memory, and ships should always be kept in working condition. Should you find that your ship needs repairing—or that you simply need a new one after that last shipwreck—seek help from a nearby island immediately.

I hope my advice proves valuable to those who seek a sailing adventure. But if you're the type who finds it tedious to spend an entire day on a boat, and the only river you're interested in crossing is the famous and frightening Styx, grab a torch and some sacrificial ram's blood, because we're headed to . . .

ᘓ THE REALMS OF THE DEAD ᘗ

Think back to your childhood. When you were a kid—jumping out of trees and engaging in other reckless behaviors that marked your future as a warrior—your worried parents likely reminded you that the trip to Hades was a one-way journey. Well, revel in the knowledge that Old Chiron's about to impart: Your parents were wrong again! Many heroes travel to the realms of the dead and survive the journey. What's more, some of them even bring back souvenirs to prove it! Pay close attention to what follows, and you, too, can add visits with the shades to your resume. Guiding you through the underworld isn't as simple as drawing a map with an arrow pointing toward the wandering souls. In fact, the term *Underworld* is a bit of a stretch! While some heroes have gone underground and knocked on Hades' door, Odysseus took a different route. He traveled due west until he reached the edge of the world. However you choose to get there (I recommend asking for directions), there are a few items and beings of note you'll need to watch out for on your journey.

⇥ STOP #1: MEET THE GUY WHO COINED THE PHRASE "CROSSING OVER" ⇤

Right before you cross into the Underworld, you'll find yourself on the banks of the River Styx. Do you see the guy with the boat? That's Charon the ferryman and he is your only way across the River. He doesn't believe that death is any excuse for skipping out on the fare, so just pay the man. Since you're trying to sneak into the place and get away with it, you don't want to draw undue attention. And hey, the guy's got a boring gig, moving

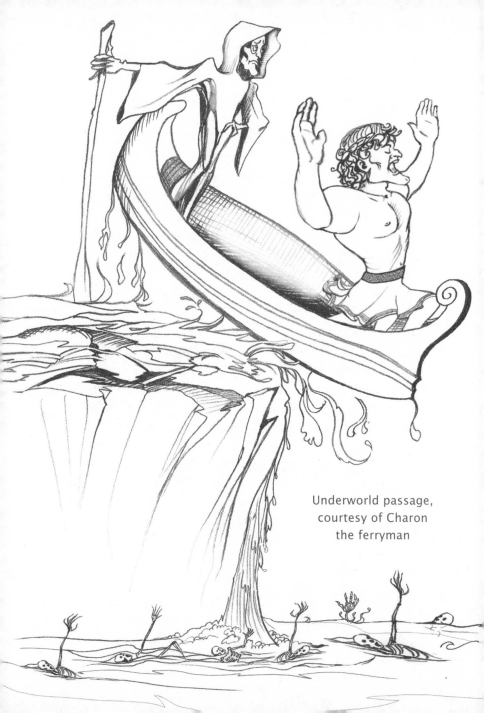

Underworld passage,
courtesy of Charon
the ferryman

soul after soul, so he probably deserves a tip. The standard fee for underworld boat travel is an *obolus* or a *danake*—loose change, really, when it comes to your rich questing purse.

→ STOP #2: BEWARE OF THE DOG, DOG, AND DOG ←

After Charon deposits you on the opposite shore, the real fun begins. The gates to Hades are guarded by Cerberus, the three-headed watchdog. Don't abandon your quest yet, he might look ominous but a dog is still a dog. Try taking a page from Orpheus's book and lull him to sleep with a lullaby on the lyre. Or, like Aeneas, simply throw him a biscuit filled with sleeping potion. Whatever you do, just get Cerberus eating *out* of your hand, rather than eating your hand. Before you know it, he'll be sleeping like a puppy, with muffled snores coming out of all three heads. Feeling *really* ambitious? Bring Cerberus home as proof of your underworld journey, or just to give your family a scare. For tips on capturing this overgrown pup, see Chapter 10. *Note*: You'll have to return him when you're done, as Hades has grown attached to his favorite hellhound over the years.

→ STOP #3: THE TORTURE TOUR ←

Sightseeing is a must in the realms of the dead. After all, this is a vacation like none other! Keep an eye out for the finer points of torture and gore.

THE WHO'S WHO OF TORTURED SOULS

SISYPHUS: See Sisyphus, punished for revealing Zeus's secrets, push a boulder up a hill, only to have it roll back down to the bottom again.

DANAIDS: Marvel as the Danaids, forty-nine beautiful husband-slayers, attempt to fill sieve-like jars full of water. It sounds like a task that takes forever . . . because it does.

TANTALUS: Watch Tantalus starve while dinner's on the table. Remember him? He was the one who turned unspeakable crimes into a family tradition.

IXION: Look for Ixion—the ancestor of Centaurs (like yours truly) by a cloud-copy of the goddess Hera (it's complicated)—nailed to a fiery wheel.

TITYOS: Catch Tityos as he literally spills his guts as the first human birdfeeder. They constantly regenerate, so he gets picked apart by winged demons ad nauseam.

Talk about tourist attractions! If you're squeamish, remember that each of the eternally condemned earned these punishments. Tantalus fed his son Pelops to the gods. Enough said? Plan an alternate route around the torture if you'd rather avoid it.

✦ STOP #4: ELYSIUM: RUBBING ELBOWS WITH THE RICH AND FAMOUS ✦

Aside from the punished and infamous, you'll also get to meet famous heroes and heroines (many of whom are featured in this very guide) during your sojourn in the Underworld. The biggest celebrities hang out in the Elysium, the good neighborhood. Make sure to go there if you want to score Achilles' autograph, but know that he'll complain about being dead. Some people never quite get over the fact that they aren't alive anymore. Prefer quieter company? Then seek out

Clouded Love: Hera and Ixion

While Zeus, as the king of the gods, has enjoyed the favors
of many a young bachelorette over the years, his wife, Hera,
doesn't get to enjoy the same privileges. Nor does Zeus take
too kindly to any competition for Hera's attention—even if it's
from losers who wouldn't be desirable in the first place.

Ixion, the king of the Lapiths, was such a guy. First, he
failed to pay the bride-price for his new wife. Then he invited
his father-in-law over to discuss the matter and offered him
a nice warm bed for the night. Unfortunately, this bed was a
touch too warm. Ixion had the bed piled with burning coals
instead of with pillows and blankets. Word of his behavior
spread and he was soon barred from most dinner parties.

For some reason, the gods were still willing to have him
as a guest, but Ixion didn't improve much upon being given
a second chance. Instead, he took the opportunity to try out
a few of his lewdest pickup lines on Hera. Zeus immediately
began to hatch a plan to make him pay for it. Indulging in
a little-known talent for sculpture, Zeus made a likeness of
Hera out of clouds, and Ixion—not noticing that Hera was a
little paler and more wispy than usual—immediately cozied
up to the cloud. The other gods caught him cuddling with
the cloud-woman (presumably laughing at Ixion's expense),
and sentenced him to special time with his fiery wheel in the
Underworld. Wicked deeds aside, it turned out that Ixion had
spent enough time with this vapor trail for the cloud-Hera
to give birth to Centauros, the father of the Centaurs. Sure,
that means I've got my share of embarrassing relatives (who
doesn't?), but without Ixion, I wouldn't be here to pass on my
heroic tips. As they say, every cloud has a silver lining.

58

⊡∏⊡∏⊡∏⊡∏⊡∏⊡∏⊡∏⊡∏⊡∏⊡∏⊡∏⊡∏

the shade of Ajax, who hasn't spoken since Odysseus screwed him out of receiving a shiny set of hand-me-down armor.

✣ STOP #5: POTENTIALLY FATAL REUNIONS? ✣

In the Underworld, you run the risk of encountering anyone who's died, including exes. Just imagine how pale Aeneas's face went when he ran into Dido, his former girlfriend, who killed herself after he left her to fend for herself in Carthage. If you run into someone you'd rather not see, you better hope that they've drunk from the forgetfulness-inducing waters of the River Lethe, so things won't be so awkward. Also, the shades have been known to wander around without remembering their former personalities, so unexpected reunions shouldn't pose a problem.

✣ DON'T LET THESE STOPS BE YOUR LAST! ✣

Finally, take heed of the number of traps that can keep you from remembering the way out of Hades, or prevent you from escaping alive. I've just talked about the waters of Lethe: The realms of the dead are strictly BYOB. Plan on bringing a boxed lunch, too. Though the local produce may look enticing, it'll soon be your only diet if you sample it. It's a well-known proverb that those who eat the food of the dead often wind up dead. Finally, if Hades or his queen Persephone offer you a chair to rest in a bit, politely decline. When Theseus attempted to carry off Persephone, he ended up chained to such a chair and wasn't able to get up until Heracles came to rescue him. (His fate after that wasn't much better, but that story is for later.)

As you can see, the Underworld has everything the discerning adventure traveler could desire, from breathtaking sights to challenges beyond the normal mortal's abilities. It's a perfect place for a hero to shine, and you'll stand out even more against the Stygian darkness. Just don't make yourself at home. Although it'd save Hermes an errand toting your soul around, you don't want to kick the bucket before your time!

Lesson Learned

Whether taking a walk in the woods or heading all the way down to Hades, remember that all trips of a heroic nature involve planning ahead! (Also, raid the farm for good gear before you embark.)

CHAPTER 6

QUEST PREP

PACKING FOR YOUR VIRGIN ADVENTURE

Your destination is set. It's now time to consider the practicalities: packing and transportation. Taking the proper supplies will help you face any situation. And securing the right vehicle is essential if you need to make a quick getaway! Here's the ultimate packing list for questing. . . .

⊰ ATTIRE ⊱

Whether you're in disguise or decked out for battle, proper heroic style is an absolute must. Here's what the polished hero sports in adventuring season:

BEGGAR'S CLOTHING: A favorite disguise for heroes who want to take back their stolen home or inheritance. As discussed earlier, if you're a hero, you're probably related to royal blood—if not to the gods themselves. Who will suspect anything when you arrive dirty and requesting table scraps? Also note that a beggar's getup is a simple-enough disguise, as rags

A well-outfitted
hero, ready for battle

are easy to come by. Need fashion advice on current styles? Talk to the Olympian seamstress, Athena. She gave Odysseus several hobo outfits for his journey home to Ithaca, and one even fooled his wife.

BREASTPLATE: A standard part of body armor, the breastplate protects your torso from both the swords of mortals and the claws of monsters. Some of the gods even wear this type of armor. Athena often sports her father's breastplate, which carries the nickname Aegis and features the head of Medusa. While yours may be a bit less ornate, this item is essential for battle.

GREAVES: This leg armor protects your lower half in war and from tusked animals like boars. Consider this, though: While useful in battle, greaves only cover the front of your legs; they don't extend toward the heel. Achilles sadly discovered this fact at Troy, when an arrow found that tender spot. Keeping this in mind, never turn your back on an enemy!

HELMET: As always, only attempt dangerous deeds with the proper protective headgear. Most helmets have eye slits for vision, so test yours first and figure out your blind spots. Some more stylish varieties come with a plume on the crest made of horsehair or feathers, which can be dyed to match your ensemble. For situations in which you have to be stealthy, see Athena about a Helmet of Invisibility.

WINGED SANDALS: Yet another fashion item that shows off Hermes' style! That said, the one pair in existence belongs to Hermes himself, so if you want to put some serious spring in your step, you'll have to borrow them. These sandals allow you to fly, and as a bonus, they'll keep you aloft when you need an extra edge in speed and agility.

TRAVELING CLOAK: Deck yourself out like the boundary-crossing god Hermes in this mantle that's both convenient and convertible. You need something to keep you warm, especially if you're heading toward the frigid North. And, when you stop on the side of the road to sleep at night, your cloak doubles as a blanket.

Chiron Enterprises takes no responsibility for misuse of divinely gifted objects and the accidents that result thereof.

WOMEN'S CLOTHING: For the ultimate disguise, dressing as the opposite sex and hiding out among the princesses works like a charm. Just remember: Your acting abilities are as important as your choice of costume. It's not enough to simply wear a dress! Learn spinning and weaving to help you better fit in among the ladies. Finally, take a few notes from Achilles' example—if you wish to remain in disguise, don't stare at any tempting piles of weapons, no matter how shiny they may appear.

⊰ WEAPONRY ⊱

There's more than one way to kill a Chimaera. In the next section, we'll go through all the possible strategies for killing monsters, but in the meantime, here are weapons to slay the beasts.

BOW AND ARROWS: Some might condemn this weapon as cowardly due to the distance it allows, but how else are you going to take down winged opponents like the Harpies? Plus your signature archery style may help identify you, if you're away from home twenty years and presumed dead in the interim. Arrows can also be made more deadly by dipping them into something poisonous before launch. The best poisons come from the monsters you slay, so be sure to stock up on a healthy supply of death-dipped darts.

CLUB: A favorite of Heracles, this simple weapon works well against opponents who require percussive encouragement. Any large block of wood will do, but feel free to whittle a handle that fits your hero-size hands. Borrowing someone else's club may prove uncomfortable in the long-term. Be sure to practice first, learning the range of your swing so you don't accidentally take out nearby spectators who are simply cheering you on!

SHIELD: This essential piece prevents stabbing and maiming, but because it features a shiny, reflective surface, you can also use it as a mirror. The mirror comes in handy for tactical reasons, or just to check that your hair still has that artfully disheveled look. The shield is an excellent device for moving people out of your way, although we don't recommend it for heavy city-state traffic. What's more, since shields are so often engraved with powerful images, they're good for decorating your palace as well as protecting you in battle, whether it contains images of your illustrious fate, or simply terrifying faces to hopefully scare your opponent to death.

SPEAR: Great for stabbing and maiming your opponent, a spear is often more useful than a sword in combat with large creatures like boars. Use a spear to land consistent jabs or hurl it from a short, safe distance.

SWORD: Like the spear, the sword was made for gashing and puncturing. Use this weapon to slice and dice your opponent's limbs or take that head right off! Keep it sharp at all times, and also keep it clean. Remember: A shiny sword is a nasty weapon. Always hold your weapon by the handle, *not* by the point. Keep the business end pointed away from yourself and toward the vital organs of your enemy.

⇥ GOODIES ⇤

What we've covered before are merely the must-haves of the heroic business. You may find, however, that you want some little extras to keep your quest running smoother. For the discerning young explorer, we recommend the following:

HELPFUL PRINCESS: Skilled at spinning and magical spells, ready to betray her overbearing father who's getting in your way—all that, and easy on the eyes, too! The ultimate tour guide to her native land, a princess knows how to pick all of the locks. Bonus: She'll usually be willing to follow you home once you've finished your quest.

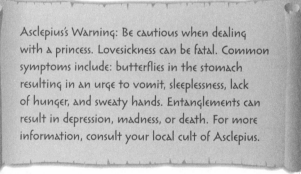

Asclepius's Warning: Be cautious when dealing with a princess. Lovesickness can be fatal. Common symptoms include: butterflies in the stomach resulting in an urge to vomit, sleeplessness, lack of hunger, and sweaty hands. Entanglements can result in depression, madness, or death. For more information, consult your local cult of Asclepius.

KIBISIS: A small leather pouch for carrying dangerous objects back from questing. Served Perseus well for toting the head of Medusa (his journey would have stopped stone-cold in its tracks were it out in the open). Usually available from the god Hermes once you win his trust.

NECTAR AND AMBROSIA: Quite literally, the choice food and drink of immortals. Mortal heroes such as yourself will want to stick to whatever you catch while hunting, but nectar and ambrosia can give you the extra energy boost you need to complete your most epic task. Give a shout to your divine relations, and they'll be sure to serve up the snack that keeps you going.

⊰ TRANSPORTATION ⊱

If you want to be a hero on the go, you'll need a way to do all of that going back and forth. Fortunately, there's a mode of transportation available for every last one of the places I've told you about:

CHARIOT: While used more for altercations in battle than for monster-slaying situations, a chariot is a handy thing and driving skills are important for young heroes. As an added bonus, you can race against your friends during your downtime and win some sweet prizes. Chariot-driving skills can also help you win a wife, as Pelops did when he raced against King Oenomaus for Hippodameia's hand. What's more, if you're a truly special hero, you can even acquire talking horses like Achilles' for your ride!

RAFT: Though lacking the style of the trireme, the raft is handy in emergency situations, such as escaping an island where a clingy goddess is holding you hostage. Make sure you're able to build one, and also that you're able to swim the rest of the way to shore in case Poseidon creates an impromptu shipwreck.

TALKING HORSES: These prized steeds dole out useful advice that may prevent you from engaging in reckless deeds.

TRIREME: A sailing vessel, the trireme is the best way to traverse the Aegean. Not meant for the hero who chooses to go solo, the trireme accommodates a big crew. So why not assemble an all-star collection of heroes? (Be warned, you'll all have to take turns rowing.) Some high-end triremes, such as Jason's *Argo*, grant wishes and come with a talking compass. To arrange for your very own talking trireme, do your best to charm Hera. Good luck with that.

YOUR OWN TWO FEET: No shame in a classic! Many a hero has gotten where he needs to be by putting one foot in front of the other. Just make sure you know where you are when traveling in treacherous terrain.

⇜ READY, SET . . . QUEST! ⇝

Now that you're geared up and you've got a rough travel plan, it's time to get to the meat of this hero business: questing. I've been watching you snooze through the family tree and geography lessons, hoping I'd finally get to the good stuff. Well, here it comes!

Questing takes a number of forms. Sometimes it's as simple as finding a monster that's terrorizing locals, slaying it, and mounting its head on the wall. Other times, you'll need to locate prized items to return to their rightful kingdoms—or place in your trophy room. You could also go to war, where green heroes become seasoned fighters, and bring back all sorts of prizes and glory.

But let me give you a final warning: If you set out to slay a monster only to find that it's already been done, don't let that stop your quest. Instead, use the tactics you've learned to scare up new monsters. Believe me, they're around. Because if there's anything the gods enjoy, it's creating strange beasts to baffle and harass mortals.

Lesson Learned

The first step in any journey is packing your bags—make sure yours aren't full of useless junk!

69

CHOOSE YOUR OWN ADVENTURE

CHAPTER 7

MONSTER MADNESS

MAN VS. BEAST

M onsters can trick even the craftiest hero. They regularly defy the laws of nature by doing stuff like attaching the head of a bull to the body of a man or by breathing fire—and who's to say they'll stay dead once slain? The previously killed Lernean Hydra could show up in your backyard tomorrow, which bodes well for your chosen career. The world will always need heroes.

There's no shortage of monsters, but the question is, which should you target? Some heroes kill just one big one and make a name for themselves, while overachieving heroes—I'm talking about you, Heracles—slay as many as mortally possible. (Go for the Marathon Approach to impress royal courtesans and daring damsels.) Ultimately, you get to choose the quest that best suits you. Now I'll review the various types of monsters and villains you'll encounter on your journey and provide a step-by-step guide on how to rid the world of their particular brand of evil.

⊰ NOT YOUR AVERAGE MENAGERIE ⊱

While the domesticated bulls, birds, and horses on your father's farm are pretty mellow, the monstrous beasts in the wild fall into a whole other category of animal. These large, frightening creatures cause many a hero to quake in his sandals. But no worries, Chiron Enterprises is here to help.

⇥ NEMEAN LION ⇤

STRENGTHS: Its soft fur is impenetrable, which means the usual weapons such as an arrow, sword, or spear will yield futile results. But the fur that makes it so difficult to kill is exactly the reason heroes are drawn to trying. Imagine wearing that fur into battle—you'd be unstoppable! Besides, it makes the ultimate fashion statement (sometimes even heroes like getting dressed to the nines).

WEAKNESSES: Still liable to the usual mortal constraints such as the need for breathing.

74

LOCATION: Nemea, in the Peloponnese.

Option #1: Wrestling

If at all possible, try and contort the beast so its own claws, the only thing that can cut through its fur, line up with its vital regions. Be careful though; wrestling a lion is not as simple as it may sound.

A hero who captures the
Nemean lion gets glory—
and great armor!

Option #2: Hanging

Look beyond stabbing to kill this lucky lion. After all, Heracles strangled him with his bare hands. If you aren't that strong, devise a way to use your farming skills. Remember how your father taught you to tie a rope and lasso the livestock? Amplify that skill by creating a noose to cut off the creature's air supply. Pull the rope back as hard as you can, until the lion has breathed his last.

Option #3: Choice Desserts

Clever heroes pick their poison (and lions almost always take the bait). From your sacrificial offering to the gods (for protection on your quest), take a bit of raw meat and garnish it with poisoned plants. Lay the tainted meat before the dwelling of the lion, and simply wait for him to have his last meal.

Once you have conquered the beast, make the most out of him. Those sharp claws will become useful in many ways. They are great tools for skinning the beast to make your fancy new cape. Also, unlike normal knives, these nails never dull. As long as you didn't go with Option #3, the lion steak will taste great with a nice red wine. But don't forget to make an offering to the gods for their help! (They love to claim all the credit.)

→ GIANT BOARS ←

STRENGTHS: Huge, heavy, and heavily tusked. These guys will tear up a garden faster than you can swing your sword.

WEAKNESSES: Mortal, and not too smart.

LOCATION: Calydon; Mount Erymanthus.

It's hard to believe that the giant boar is a great cousin to the piglets on your farm. Boars and beasts of that ilk roam the land freely; most are sent by a pissed-off Artemis. The hunting goddess sent King Oeneus the Calydonian Boar (a huge beast) to ravage his lands because he forgot to make an annual sacrifice to her. These creatures destroy vineyards and other crops, and scare peasants out of their homes. Extra-large, heavy, and with large tusks, it's no wonder normal men fear them. But it falls to a hero—the best of men—to rid the world of these gigantic porkers. Read the tales of two swine, and the heroes who stuck them.

FOR YOUR BOARING RELATIVE, THE EURYMANTHIAN PORKER

When Heracles came to me for advice on capturing the Eurymanthian Boar, I advised him (over a bottle of Dionysus's finest wine) to drive the beast into a snowbank. Its weight would sink its hoofs and tusks into the snow, thus immobilizing the animal. Then Heracles merely had to bind it and carry it back to his fearful uncle. (The uncle Eurystheus that sent Heracles on his quests was a big coward that would hide whenever his nephew returned victoriously carrying a fearsome beast.)

HUNTING FOR THE WHOLE HOG: THE CALYDONIAN BOAR HUNT

Meleager's more formidable task was to kill the Calydonian Boar. To off the pudgy porcine, he gathered a hunting party of the best heroes, a real who's who of the bravest men (and woman) in Greece. While many fought valiantly, a few, ahem, Nestor, chose to hide in trees. (Note: For a successful hunting trip, pick only the most courageous companions.) I don't recommend swords for this particular battle; the tusks of the beast are sharp, and its bristles are like prickly spikes. Instead, to keep your hog in place shoot an arrow into its small red eye. Ask the best archer to deliver this blow. Once blinded, the boar may become even more violent, but at least it won't be able to see your attacks. You can't reach its vital organs, so stab your spears deep into its shoulder and back to kill it. Then be sure to sacrifice to Artemis!

BYOS (BRING YOUR OWN SPEAR: A DIFFERENT KIND OF PARTY)

The Calydonian Boar was such a problem for the countryside, Meleager needed all the strength Greece had to offer. Over thirty heroes joined in on the action, including some of the most notable names. The heroes Jason, Theseus (with his ever-constant sidekick Pirithous), and Atalanta definitely stand out on the list. However some of the lesser-knowns fathered some of the next generation of heroes including Peleus, the father of Achilles; Laertes, the father of Odysseus; and Telamon, the father of Ajax. The twin Dioscuroi, Helen's brothers Castor and Polydeuces, also joined the party. Heracles' buddy Admetus also joined the wise Nestor to defeat this ham of a beast. Meleager also invited his uncles, Toxeus and Plexippus, which turned out to be a bad decision. After the boar was killed, Meleager's relatives were quite irate at his choice to give the spoils to the pretty Atalanta, and the feud that resulted later cost the uncles and Meleager their lives.

✦ STYMPHALIAN BIRDS ✦

STRENGTHS: The most ferocious of birds the world has to offer, these nasty avian warriors were designed for battle, with wings that fire arrows, and beaks that can pierce even the strongest armor.

WEAKNESSES: Mortal and birdbrained.

LOCATION: Lake Stymphalia, Arcadia.

Yep, they sure can mess you up, but fortunately their defenses aren't so hot. To slay them, you've got to first drive them out of their trees. Do this by clanging castanets like Heracles did or simply by making a racket. Then aim and shoot to take them down with your bow and arrow.

✦ FIRE-BREATHING BULLS ✦

STRENGTHS: Breathe fire.

WEAKNESSES: Smoker's cough.

LOCATION: Colchis.

79

On his quest for the Golden Fleece, Jason needed to complete a strange task: He had to yoke two fire-breathing bulls together. If you end up in a similar bind, or have to snuff out some blazing beasts (i.e., the Chimaera or Cacus), trust this strategy:

STEP #1: Find a witch, or a beautiful princess who can cast spells. She should be able to whip up a magic ointment to protect you from flames. (I'd give you the recipe, but all self-respecting heroes leave the cooking to the women.)

STEP #2: Apply ointment thirty minutes before confronting the smoking steeds so it fully soaks into your skin. Also apply it to your sword and shield to make the metal heat-resistant.

STEP #3: Once you and your gear are set, slay the beasts as you would any standard cattle. Slit their throats, and then prepare a lovely feast.

The benefit of fire-breathing creatures is that their meat is already partially cooked. Serve the bull with ice-cold beer.

Lesson Learned

No matter the size of the animal, or its extra protective enhancements, the key to being a hero is planning ahead. Now that you know the step-by-step process, you can go out and rid the world of giant pigs or fire-breathing bulls! (But never underestimate your enemy.)

CHAPTER
8

MONSTER MASH

FREAKS AND GREEKS

The monsters of this category will blow your mind. They range from simple hybrids to extreme genetic anomalies. Here, we'll travel through the world of strange creatures with even stranger bodies so you'll have a clue about how to slay them.

→ MEDUSA ←

STRENGTHS: Has the power to turn people into stone, with just one glance.

WEAKNESSES: Only one in her family subject to the problem of mortality.

LOCATION: North Africa.

For some monsters you encounter in your journey, a simple, one-stroke stabbing will suffice. Others require more gear. So, make like a Boy Scout, and *be prepared*—especially when you're facing the likes of Medusa.

Of the frightful, snake-hair Gorgon Sisters, only Medusa is susceptible to death. Imagine her head in your trophy room—quite a feat for a newbie hero! What's more, her head can be used as a weapon for turning bullies to stone. But, slayer beware: Medusa's glare can kill, and without the proper equipment, you may end up as a statue. To avoid that cruel fate, you'll want to pack this stuff for your journey to the ends of the earth:

One (1) cap of invisibility

One (1) sickle, a curved blade used in agriculture

One (1) bag for head-storage purposes

One (1) polished shield, the more reflective the better

One (1) pair winged sandals

> Make sure you practice before using any of these items! Chiron Enterprises takes no responsibility for accidents involving flying footwear.

Wait until all three Gorgons are asleep before initiating your attack. To maximize the stealth factor, don your cap of invisibility and winged sandals. Keep eyes away from target while approaching. Use reflection of target in shield to properly align sickle with target's jugular. Remember: Shields are concave, so the image may be inverted. Slice cleanly, keeping utmost caution around serpentine hair follicles. Deposit severed head in bag. Exit before target's sisters can enact vengeance.

→ THE MINOTAUR ←

STRENGTHS: This man-eating beast has the strength and anger of a bull, with the sharp horns to match.

WEAKNESSES: Those heavy horns cause him to be a bit top-heavy, so once thrown off balance, he's far easier to slay. Plus, his vital organs are encased in the man-half of his body, so his thick hide is really just for show.

LOCATION: Labyrinth in the basement of King Minos's palace, Knossos, Crete.

When killing monsters, sometimes the act of slaying is the easy part, while finding the beast and getting out alive is the tricky part. Take the Minotaur of the Cretan Labyrinth, for example. While the Minotaur's body isn't complex—he's half man, half bull—his labyrinth, designed for King Minos by Daedalus, makes me dizzy just thinking about it. Some tips to navigate your way through the Minotaur's tangled lair:

Option #1: Learn the Layout

Sneak into Daedalus's workshop, find the blueprints to the labyrinth, and memorize them. But know that this option has its flaws. Daedalus is crafty—and he's just the sort of jerk to leave out fake blueprints to throw you off. How can you be sure you've found the real thing? If Daedalus has already flown the coop, he probably took the plans with him or destroyed them ahead of time.

Option #2: Thread Your Way

Bring your own piece of yarn and use it to mark your path. String is an essential piece of any heroic toolkit, and . . . hell-o.

This is a test of heroic skill. What are you doing, crocheting on the job? What do you need yarn for? Be a man!

Option #3: One Part Good Looks, One Part Charm, All Hero (The Best Option)

Charm the king's daughter with your winning good looks. (Try brushing your hair ahead of time.) She'll give you a bit of yarn from her craft bag, and you'll be able to retain your manly reputation. Don't get your hopes up for a committed relationship—you *are* killing her half-brother, after all. Enter the labyrinth and tie the end of the string to the entrance pillar. Keep the string with you to mark where you've been, and follow the stench to the Minotaur.

Once you've found him (by way of blueprints or string), a single sword to the gut should do it. If you really want to get fancy, take a cue from Crete's most popular sport, Extreme Bull-Leaping. Jump, grab the Minotaur by the horns, and vault over his back before dealing the fatal blow. That shows pizzazz.

⇾ THE SPHINX ⇽

STRENGTHS: This flying lioness has a taste for the idiots of Greece.

WEAKNESSES: Sore loser who can't stand not being the smartest creature in the room.

LOCATION: Cliffside on the path to Thebes.

The Sphinx will do the work for *you*. . . . That is, if you grant her this one favor. You see, she's an inquisitive little beast—part human, part lion, and graced with the little wings of a bird—

who's got a penchant for puzzling passersby. Answer her riddle correctly and she'll kill herself on the spot. Answer incorrectly, and you're the main course.

Some say the Sphinx's ultimate goal is to weed out the idiot savants from the idiots, so if you plan to go up against her, you need to keep your brain in shape. Practice daily with an approved heroic riddle-book such as *Classic Puzzles for the Mind's Eye* by Oedipus.

In the meantime, you can practice with a few of the Sphinx's favorites:

QUESTION: What goes on four in the morning, two at midday, three at night, but is strongest when it goes on the fewest?

Answer: Man

QUESTION: What has eyes on the bottom, ears on the top, and dancing women all around it?

Answer: A drinking cup

QUESTION: I either smile or frown, but I can't do both. I have no eyes but when I look out I see much watching me back.

Answer: A mask

Note: Any answers to the riddle of the Sphinx may return to later unravel your life.

✦ CHIMAERA ✦

STRENGTHS: As a combination of a lion, a snake, and a goat, she has all of these various animals' strengths including speed, venom, and ferocity. Oh, and she breathes fire.

85

WEAKNESSES: With so many animal attachments, the Chimaera is never entirely sure which body part to use to start an attack. Plus, fires can always be extinguished!

LOCATION: Lycia, in Asia Minor.

A lion with a snake's tail and a goat's head growing out of her back, the Chimaera practically defines a hybrid monster. Oh—and this "she-goat" spews fire. As the mother of the Sphinx and the Nemean Lion, you've got to wonder about her family background. . . . To kill this oddball beast, shoot her from above to avoid her many heads and burning breath. Or, tip your spear with a lump of lead that will melt when exposed to the Chimaera's fiery breath; follow the spear thrust by stabbing her from above. Aim for the throat to keep her from frying you.

→ ARGUS ←

STRENGTHS: This ever-vigilant beast has one hundred eyes, which makes it tough for anything to get by him.

WEAKNESSES: Can't resist a lullaby (and can't sleep with his eyes open!).

LOCATION: Temple of Hera in Argos.

As queen of the gods, Hera knows how to pick an excellent sentry. She employs Argus, this all-seeing sentinel, to protect whatever she wants to keep from her husband, from birthday gifts to personal vices.

Argus will see your every approach unless you can get him to close all of his eyes. There are a few options, some better than others. For example, everyone closes their eyes when they sneeze, but it's unlikely you'll be able to pull this off from a distance for a long enough period to gain an advantage.

Instead, brush up on your music skills. Like Orpheus and Achilles, the best heroes know how to rock out. Compose a lullaby, preferably before going on your quest. This way, you'll have time to practice the tune so that the trick works. Lull the many-eyed monster to sleep with this slow, sweet melody, and once all of his eyes have closed in deep sleep, slice off his head. Then you can help yourself to the loot he was guarding.

Note: Use the song you compose for Argus to soothe angry relatives or irate deities.

→ CETO ←

STRENGTHS: Her venomous blood means that every drop she drips can kill you instantly! Plus, those snaky coils adorning her head aren't just for decoration.

WEAKNESSES: Her large size causes Ceto to move slowly, which means any agile hero can easily sneak past.

LOCATION: Off the coast of Jaffa, on the Ethiopian shoreline.

Your antennae should go up anytime you see a maiden chained to a rock by the sea; it's a sure sign that something's lying just offshore. Take Ceto, for example, a giant sea creature with a large neck and a head crowned with poisonous vipers. She's got venomous blood, so you must be careful of how you kill this beast.

Hermes' winged sandals (which you used while slaying Medusa) come in handy because flying allows the best vantage point for the kill. In fact, if you're journeying back from slaying the Gorgon, you could use her monstrous head to turn Ceto to stone. But then the beast will sink to the bottom of the ocean, which means no trophy for you. What's the point of that? Instead, follow these simple steps:

1. Get airborne, via sandals or flying horse, and be prepared to move fast.
2. Stab Ceto in her large neck, far from her snaky head, which will render her head useless as a weapon.
3. Stab her in the back and the ribs to complete the kill.
4. Take a leafy blanket of seaweed and lay it on Ceto's head. This living, absorbent foliage will soak up the monster's deadly blood and will turn it into rock.

Your creature-to-coral transformation will entertain nearby nymphs and add to the natural sea scenery.

→LERNEAN HYDRA←

STRENGTHS: Never loses her heads in battle.

WEAKNESSES: Can't have a hot head.

LOCATION: Lernean Swamps, southeast of Mycenae.

A seven-headed water serpent with a giant crab for a best friend, the Hydra is a tricky mutant to defeat. If her many heads weren't freaky enough, watch out for her coils that will slither from the water to grab you as you come near. You must rely on speed and agility to beat this beast. Her sidekick, the crabby crustacean, will do anything to defend her, and poses yet another obstacle.

Phase #1: Terminating the Crab Clause

First, get rid of the sidekick. Remember crabbing with your family on that nice afternoon in Crete? Same rules apply here. First, create a large net (and I mean large—this crab is huge!) with super-strong rope. Lure the crab with some tasty meat, then grab him with the net. Hang the net in a tall tree—once you've finished off the Hydra, you can celebrate with a raucous crab-bake.

Phase #2: Heads Up!

Now on to the main event. To prevent the Hydra from grabbing your legs, you'll want to cut the coils—and quickly (they move fast!). Her heads cause the real headache. No wonder the Hydra has just one friend. Her breath is absolutely foul, fatal even. And beheading her is pointless since another swiftly appears in its place. Try this workaround:

1. Begin hacking off the Hydra's heads.
2. Cauterize her headless stumps after each decapitation. This prevents six of the heads from growing back.
3. Attack the seventh—her main brain. Cut it off and squash it under a rock. This prevents her mind and body from working together against you.
4. Stab her in the ribs to finish her off.

To get the job done, employ your *own* sidekick who will do the cauterizing while you complete the decapitation. Any young, eager, wannabe hero can assist. (You must have a relative who's willing to tag along? Honestly, most boys are pyromaniacs anyway.)

89

Heracles asked his nephew Iolaus to help him out when he fought the Hydra. A few words of caution: Watch your exposure to blood during the attack. More deadly than her breath, the Hydra's blood can kill in an instant. The upside? The poison helps pimp your weapons. But beware, as this can backfire. Heracles found this out the hard way, when he was accidentally killed by his wife, using a potion that contained the Hydra's blood.

Dynamic Duos: Sometimes It Takes Two!

Heracles wasn't the only hero to recruit a sidekick, when he used his nephew Iolaus's hands to help him out with the Hydra. Many heroes have had best friends accompany them on their quests (after all, traveling with a buddy is more fun!):

THESEUS accomplished great deeds with Pirithous, until Pirithous got stuck lounging on the job in the underworld. (See Chapter 13, on Reunion Tours, for more on that.)

ODYSSEUS often employed the help of his good friend Diomedes as they snuck around to sack Troy.

THE GREAT HERO ACHILLES enjoyed having his sidekick Patroclus nearby, even if it was just to cook him dinner.

Traveling with a buddy makes any quest more fun!

✦ GERYON AND ORTHUS ✦

STRENGTHS: Geryon is an amazing fighter, with six fists ready to fly in your face.

WEAKNESSES: While all the extra limbs are handy, those extra hands often get tangled. Take advantage of this! Plus, only having two legs means the bottom half is far easier to defeat.

LOCATION: The island of Erytheia, near the Hesperides, at the far western end of the Mediterranean.

Once upon a time there was a bizarre-looking giant and his equally strange-looking pet dog. If you think that sounds like an excellent opening for a kids' story, think again. Geryon, grandson of Medusa, has three bodies joined at the waist—six arms and three heads! Somehow, he got away with only having two legs. His constant companion is a two-headed puppy named Orthus, with twice the number of teeth for going after unlucky messengers. These genetic anomalies work together to guard the Cattle of the Sun, and make for an interesting kill.

Focus on the canine first; he's easy to get out of the way. Simply bash his two heads together with the right amount of force, and *wham!* No more guard dog. To slay his owner, try using the arrows laced with the venomous blood of the Lernean Hydra. Or, for an even easier kill, shoot him in the legs to render him immobile. This way you can save your valuable arrows. You can also slice off his heads or stab him in each of his hearts while the poison slowly works its way through his lower extremities.

→ CACUS ←

STRENGTHS: Breathes fire. Which means he can always turn you into a nice medium-rare meal.

WEAKNESSES: Can't wash down his meal with a drink, or else his fire will go out.

LOCATION: A cave on the Aventine Hill in Italy.

If in the course of your questing you find yourself herding cattle in Italy—you never know, it could be fun—keep close watch on your herd around the Aventine Hill. In a cave nearby lives a three-headed, fire-breathing monster whose favorite pastime is cattle rustling. Since the flock of a hero has to be something special, such as the Cattle of the Sun that Geryon guards, this rural ravager may make you his next target. What's more, he gets creative with leftovers and uses them as exterior decorations. Granted, his favorite dinner is human flesh, so it makes sense that he would nail the heads of his victims to the entrance of his cave. This son of Hephaestus is called Cacus, and if you choose to battle him, there are a couple of ways to go about it:

Plan Alpha

This blazing beast prefers to fight within his cave, taking advantage of the small space by filling it with smoke. This makes it difficult to see him and can turn the cave into an oven. So, jump past the fire and smoke, and make sure you hold your breath! Once you reach him, sneak up from behind quickly and quietly. Stealth is of the essence. Try to keep your arms out of the range of his flames. Next, attempt to strangle him. Or, if you have good aim, use the same method that Bellerophon used for defeating the Chimaera—put lead down her throat to keep her from creating sparks.

Plan Beta

Your next best bet? Employ the ultimate tool against a raging fire—a flood. If you have Herculean strength, you can divert the nearby Tiber River and fill his cave with water. This negates both the power and the utility of his breath, and you'll walk away cool and collected.

⇥ HARPIES ⇤

STRENGTHS: Backed by Zeus, the king of the gods. Also, their birdlike abilities mean they not only fly, they are extremely quick!

WEAKNESSES: Constantly plagued by hunger. Their low blood-sugar level means they aren't always thinking their attacks through.

LOCATION: Strophades Islands.

A mixture of bird and woman, these soaring shoplifters look pretty strange. They basically fly around stealing everything they set their eyes on. Lovely haired sisters of the messenger goddess Iris, they live in the Strophades but can be found elsewhere when doing the will of the gods.

Take this, for example: Angry at the prophetic king Phineas, Zeus blinded him and left him on an isolated island with only the Harpies for company. These women showed up just in time for dinner, quite the rude uninvited guests, and snatched his meal directly from his hands. Talk about rotten luck—they didn't even leave any leftovers!

Phineas was eventually rescued by Jason and his heroic friends, the Boreads, sons of the North Wind. Together, they shot the Harpies with arrows and captured them in a net. Phineas was so relieved that he used his oracular skill to give Jason advice for his journey. You never know what reward you will get for saving the day, but always be sure to help out the prophets! Granted, you'll also need to know how to make sense out of the prophecies, which I'm going to help you with later. A good first step, however, is making sure the prophet in question doesn't mumble too much.

In fact, the Harpies are often doing Zeus's bidding and punishing and torturing people on their way to the Underworld. Always find out why the cruel and vicious Harpies are hanging around before engaging them in battle. Otherwise, you run the risk of helping out someone who completely deserves his nasty fate. You don't want to anger Zeus!

✦ SIRENS ✦

STRENGTHS: Their beautiful voices really draw a crowd.

WEAKNESSES: Despite having wings, they can't take their music on tour, as they are stuck on their isolated island.

LOCATION: Mysterious island in the Mediterranean Sea.

Mistresses of song, these melodious women know how to lure an audience—to their own destruction. From miles away, sailors follow their enchanting voices, literally dying to hear their name in the heroes' ode. But these are no ordinary singers.

Once you get close you will see the resemblance they bear to those other wicked winged women, the Harpies. And if you're near enough to see their bird-like appearance, forget it. You are already doomed. Take my word for it. They look like Harpies.

I'm sorry to report that no hero has ever killed the Sirens. Many heroes die in the shipwrecks that occur in the ladies' less-than-approachable harbor, and once the bodies wash up on shore, the savage Sirens feast on the blood. Really, if questing takes you out to the Mediterranean often, avoid their island altogether.

However, if you wish to hear their song (personalized just for you with stories of your far-reaching fame) without dying, follow in the footsteps of Odysseus. The one time he sailed by the Sirens' concert, he ordered his crew to secure him to the mast of his ship. They then plugged their own ears with wax to protect themselves from the seductive tunes. Using this strategy, you should be able to sail safely by their rocky shores while enjoying their catchy tunes. Make sure those wax plugs work well, or you risk losing your crew! You may be a great hero, but no one can row a trireme on his own.

Chiron Enterprises is not to be held responsible for any wax earplug failure, including but limited to the resulting shipwreck and Siren dinner course of your crew. Please be sure to test out your earplugs before embarking on your adventure. If they can block out the sounds of your wife's or mother's nagging, they should do the trick.

These monsters are pretty easy to identify as foes for a very good reason: They look monstrous. In the next chapter, prepare yourself for a bit of a surprise. Not every enemy will look this way; in fact, some will look like humans. Care to learn how to take them on? Stay tuned. . . .

Lesson Learned

While hybrid beasts may combine the best of various beasts, or even have an extra hand to help them out, often these combinations wind up causing their downfall. Tremendous size makes you move slowly, multiple heads make you think less clearly, and there is always a weak spot that the clever hero can find!

9

TWO-FACED MONSTERS

DEVIOUS DEEDS, DEADLY ALLIANCES

Looks can be deceiving in the wide world of questing. Some monsters may look just like your next-door neighbor, and others may look more like your second cousin (if you squint and turn your head to the side). The following roster includes a beautiful yet destructive woman, monstrous men, and gruesome giants you could encounter in your travels. Don't assume that just because they look okay, they're on your side!

→ CIRCE ←

STRENGTHS: Wields powerful beauty and magic. Her charming home is also quite the draw for sea-weary travelers.

WEAKNESSES: Goes weak at the knees for a hero that doesn't fall for her magical charms. Has an aversion to the moly plant.

LOCATION: The island of Aeaea.

Do you need a break? Does that charming little house with smoke rising through the chimney look like the *perfect* resting place? Not so fast. The beautiful woman who lives there is just as deadly as any other monstrous beast. Do not, under any circumstances, fall for her smokin' good looks and charm. This woman, Circe, is not your standard innkeeper, but a witch who invites company over for a nice pork dinner—with her guests as the main course. If your crew doesn't get that at first, repeat it to them in plain Greek: "She is a witch who will turn you into pigs."

As a hero, your task is to turn a deadly situation into an ideal vacation. If you'll be traveling in Circe's 'hood, be sure to bring along a potion based on the moly plant, a black root with a brilliant white flower. If your local market doesn't have it, check with Hermes. He's great at scoring hard-to-find goods.

Slip this potion into *your* food, and it will neutralize her magic. But it gets better! You'll impress Circe so much with your heroic prowess that she'll fall in love with you instantly. Make her swear an oath not to harm you; after all, you are a busy hero with no time to deal with a scorned lover. Once she swears, this dangerous scene becomes an island paradise with a beautiful and magical woman by your side (one who can also give great directions for navigating the Underworld— bonus!). Enjoy your much-deserved vacation. . . .

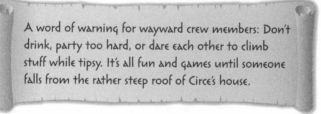

A word of warning for wayward crew members: Don't drink, party too hard, or dare each other to climb stuff while tipsy. It's all fun and games until someone falls from the rather steep roof of Circe's house.

→ CYCLOPS (POLYPHEMUS) ←

STRENGTHS: Tremendous size and the highest of connections, considering their close kinship to the gods.

WEAKNESSES: Small brains and only one eye.

LOCATION: The island of the Cyclopes, located somewhere in the Mediterranean Sea.

This one-eyed giant looks somewhat human, except in the face and size and probably smell. The Cyclopes are either the uncles of the Olympians or perhaps even their kids. (No one said divine family trees made sense!) They dwell in caves, make goat cheese, and treat their livestock like pets. Polyphemus, the Cyclops that Odysseus encountered on his travels, was quite an attentive shepherd. But these creatures don't show trespassers the same kindness they show their sheep. When humans land on their island, they'll forget their vegetarian ways in favor of devouring flesh for lunch.

If you encounter a Cyclops, it's best to give an alias and avoid revealing your true identity. As a direct offspring of the gods, you don't want him running home to his daddy, Poseidon, with the name of the hero who bullied him.

While Cyclopes are often busy making lightning bolts for Zeus or tending their sheep, fighting them tends to be less of a quest and more a matter of self-defense. To keep from being eaten, you will need to first incapacitate your Cyclops. Odysseus did this by getting Polyphemus really drunk, which takes the strongest wine that Greece has to offer. Don't water it down! Once your targeted one-eyed behemoth passes out,

99

make your attack. Odysseus, the only hero to battle a Cyclops one on one, considered these two methods.

The first: stab-and-run. But he decided he needed a bigger sword, and wasn't even positive that would kill the monster. Instead, Odysseus opted for a more creative way out. He used a burned stick to blind Polyphemus. Nowadays, this burned stick is considered the weapon of choice for taking down a Cyclops.

Warning: Try not to poke your eye out while attempting to take out someone else's!

Once you have blinded the one-eyed giant, carefully plan your escape. In this case, you're going to want to disguise yourself, so no one sees you leaving. Remember all those beloved pets that Polyphemus kept in his cave? Well, try hiding your crew under the ewes, and make sure they hold on tight. (You may want to secure them with ropes just to be safe.) As the hero, you've earned a manlier exit. You get to hide under the ram—the leader of the pack. Once the blinded Cyclops stumbles to the boulder door to let his pets out to pasture, hang on and enjoy the ride.

✦ THE GIANT ANTAEUS ✦

STRENGTHS: Adds strength to his already overgrown muscles just by touching his mother, the Earth.

WEAKNESSES: A true mama's boy, when he is separated from his mother, he loses the extra strength she provides; in other words, he's afraid of flying.

LOCATION: North Africa.

Another child of Poseidon (this one lacking affection for sheep), is the Giant Antaeus—and if having the sea for your father isn't enough, this big lug's mom is Earth herself, Gaia. His favorite pastime? Challenging unsuspecting opponents to a wrestling match. Once he claims victory, the opponent's skull becomes part of the most morbid temple to the god of the sea that the Greek world has ever seen. Not exactly a welcoming sight for tourists! As mentioned earlier, since he is a child of the Earth, he draws his strength from her and is extremely danger-ous as long as his feet are planted on the ground. The only way that you can defeat him is to rival his monstrous strength, like Heracles did. Those of you with mere normal strength and no chance for divine intervention may want to sit this one out. But the rest of you need to hold Antaeus off the ground. This will keep him from renewing his strength and beating you. Once his feet are dangling in the air, squeeze the life out of him with a menacing hug.

Note: Giants may try to eat you. They find humans far tastier than any sheep, cow, or goat. Try not to look as if you'd be tasty with tzatziki and a side of pita; that should keep you from becoming the main course.

→ PROCRUSTES ←

STRENGTHS: Not really a strength, but this clever keeper only attacks his guests when they are sleeping so they won't fight back. Many fall victim to his "innocent innkeeper" act.

WEAKNESSES: Despite immense cruelty, he is still just a puny mortal.

LOCATION: Mount Korydallos (located on the sacred way between Athens and Eleusis).

Some of the nastiness you encounter on your quest won't take the form of monsters or witches. Humans can be every bit as cruel. Take someone like Procrustes, for example. This ruthless innkeeper offers two rooms in his lodging, one with a king-size bed and the other with a small cot. Oddly, he prefers to place his taller guests in the smaller bed and his shorter guests in the larger one.

What gives? Under the pretense of hospitality, Procrustes claims he wants his guest to fit the bed perfectly, and goes to cruel extremes to balance out these sleeping arrangements. For the larger guest, he cuts off parts that don't fit on the small cot, while he gets a morbid glee out of stretching the body of his petite guest to fit the longer bed.

When dealing with bloodthirsty humans, all you can do is give them a taste of their own medicine. Let's look at the strategies of Theseus, who defeated Procrustes the first time. First, ask Procrustes if he'll demonstrate the size and comfort of the bed before you test it out yourself. Once he is in the bed, give him the same treatment he gives his guests: Start hacking or stretching away. If you decide to still crash at the inn, I suggest teaching Procrustes his lesson in the cot, so you can sleep soundly in the bed sized for the king that you will surely become at the end of your journeys.

⇸ SINIS ⇷

STRENGTHS: Innovative in his pickpocket strategies.

WEAKNESSES: Still just a human, no matter how mean.

LOCATION: At the Isthmus of Corinth.

This thief awaits all travelers on the path to the Isthmus, ready to stir up trouble. But Sinis isn't content with a simple mugging. After defeating his victim in a fistfight, this twisted dude ties

Pray for No Vacancy!

While traveling around the Mediterranean, ridding the world of monsters and villains, heroes need to be selective about sleeping arrangements. Although a good night's rest in a cozy bed sounds divine, that rock you were using as a pillow may trump the treatment you'll receive from some inhospitable innkeepers. Here are the inns you'll want to avoid like the plague:

CIRCE'S ISLE INN: While this beautiful woman tends a charming home, steer clear of this witch's brews!

CALYPSO'S ISLAND RETREAT: Located on a beautiful beach front, at first you will never want to leave this paradise. And trust me, she will never let you!

PROCRUSTES BUNK: This inn always has vacancies, but the blood by the beds should pretty much explain why. (See Procrustes notes, page 101.)

his defeated opponent to two pine trees that he has pinned to the ground. Once Sinis lets go, the trees swing up and rip his victim in half, sending limbs flying. As his unfortunate prey flies through the air, Sinis gathers the coins that fall from his pockets and purses. A true bully, this man needs a taste of his own medicine. And you—like Theseus—are just the guy to do it!

Teach Sinis this lesson once and he'll quit harassing innocent folks. Now, defeating a regular human should not be too difficult for the likes of you—especially as you've probably killed a slew of beasts and monsters by this point. Just don't get too cocky! Once you have wrestled Sinis to the ground, tie him to the two trees and then let the trunks go. As his body is carried toward the sky, his soul will realize the error of his ways on his journey to the Underworld.

✦ SCIRON AND HIS MAN-EATING TORTOISE ✦

STRENGTHS: Location, location, location. Positions himself in a high-traffic place with a nice cliff nearby to dispose of the bodies.

WEAKNESSES: Compared to a great hero like you, this stinky mortal is just scrawny.

LOCATION: Near Megara.

Another robber on your path has a thing for strangers washing his feet. This strange man will force travelers to kneel before him and scrub his skanky toes. As if that's not nasty enough, Sciron has a deadlier scheme up his sleeve. Once the unlucky traveler has started the foot rub, Sciron kicks them off the cliff, turning him into pet food for his giant tortoise. He's just

A cunning hero gives Sciron a taste of his own medicine

BEWARE OF MAN-EATING TORTOISE

another cruel human, in the ranks of Sinis and Procrustes, so we'll punish him in the same manner. After all your travels, wouldn't a nice foot massage be well-deserved? Defeat this puny human in a wrestling match, and then hold out your tired and sweaty (but still heroic and attractive) feet for the bath. Make sure you're wearing your old sandals and have picked up a lot of dirt along the way. Just to psych him out, you may want to wait until he has almost completed his task before kicking him to the tortoise.

✦ EARTHBORN WARRIORS ✦

STRENGTHS: Born from the ground, they can spring up anywhere at any time. Plus their mother, the Earth, already equips them with weapons, so they are born ready for a fight!

WEAKNESSES: Like Antaeus the Giant, they need the aid that their mother Earth provides (they're also afraid of being airborne. . . .).

LOCATION: Can appear anywhere on Earth, but spotted in Thebes and Colchis so far.

If you face a small army of men and it seems like the enemy's forces are coming out of nowhere, you may be fighting the Sparti, or other earthborn warriors. Essentially these men of mud spring up from Earth itself, brandishing special weapons made of Gaia's own ore.

Trying to kill them on their own turf is not recommended. When you get tired, it might be time for a change in strategy. Either draw them out to sea or onto a place not connected to the earth. Once you have slain a Sparti, or other earthborn warrior, do not let his body touch the ground; otherwise, he'll come back to life. Remember, he is much like the Giant Antaeus. Keep the Sparti's body suspended in a tree, for example, so that their numbers dwindle until you have defeated the army.

Lesson Learned

A good hero never gives his trust willingly. Keep your guard up while traveling and beware the beauties. Any mortal, or person who appears human, could be out to get you. Wouldn't you rather be known for being killed by a multi-headed, fire-breathing vicious monster than some pretty waif or innkeeper?

CURIOUS QUESTS

LOFTY LABORS AND TAME TASKS

M aybe killing a creature isn't all it's cracked up to be. Maybe you want some reward for your work, other than just the gratitude of a town freed from fear. Well, you've come to the right place, because wise old Chiron is here to point you to your dream quest. From heading out on a scavenger hunt for rare objects to extreme do-gooder excursions, these quests promise to offer something more gratifying.

109

❧ HIDE AND GO FLEECE ❧

If killing mythical creatures isn't your thing—perhaps you're not a big fan of blood, or you just can't help seeing your puppy at home every time you look at a hybrid—you can always go for the scavenger hunt–style quest. With this option, you just capture the beast and bring it home for show-and-tell. (Of course, in your attempt to keep the creature alive and tame— no easy task—you may decide that killing it would have been easier.) Here we review animals to fetch rather than kill (i.e., a favored pet of a god, because at this point we know how easy it is to incur the wrath of the immortals), but also some enchanted objects that'll look impressive hanging by your hearth.

→ TRAP THE CERYNEIAN DEER ←

TASK DIFFICULTY: ☠ ☠ ☠

The Ceryneian Deer, Artemis's favorite pet, is a truly remarkable creature to find in the wild. You can cash in this doe's golden antlers for bank. Well-accessorized with brazen hooves to match, this deer gives you something awe-inspiring to display for your evil relatives, or that teacher who said you'd never amount to anything.

But because she is Artemis's pet, you *absolutely* have to get permission. If you ask really nicely and offer her a fantastic sacrifice, Artemis may lend it to you for a week or so. But since she's the goddess of the hunt, she won't just hand it over on a leash. You'll have to prove your skills first. Before you can even ask to borrow the deer, you'll have to capture it.

1. Deer are skittish creatures, and startle easily at the slightest sound. This makes your task a lot harder, so don't wear clunky sandals and approach with a soft step.
2. Think twice about wounding the deer. When Heracles captured the Ceryneian Deer, he shot her near the leg and wounded her slightly. That said, while *he* got away with it, you won't. Most gods consider him an exception to the rules.
3. Instead, set some humane traps. Tie a net to a tree and disguise the net with leaf cover. Then try to drive the deer into

the net. Then you'll be sure it's coming home completely unscathed.

Once captured, take good care of Artemis's beloved pet and return her in pristine condition. If injured or mistreated in any way, you can add Artemis to the list of the gods against you. And you don't want Artemis angry at you—if she's feeling generous, she'll turn you into one of the game she likes to chase, and your *hunting* days will suddenly become your *hunted* days.

✦ TAME THE MARES OF DIOMEDES ✦

TASK DIFFICULTY: ☠ ☠ ☠ ☠

If you think fetching one animal is tough, capturing the four Thracian horses of Diomedes is exponentially tougher. Podagros (The Fast), Lampon (The Shining), Xanthos (The Blonde), and Deinos (The Terrible) are fire-breathing, man-eating horses, each of whom live up to their name—and then some. They're owned by a giant named Diomedes (no relation to the Diomedes of the Trojan War we're going to hear about later). This formidable son of Ares could barely control these wild horses on his own, which might make your task seem a bit more difficult. But I'm sure you're up for the challenge.

First, apply that fire-resistant lotion to protect you from the horses' blazing breath. You'll be glad you did. While the lotion settles in, fight off the horses' master so he doesn't get in your way. Remember: Killing a giant requires cunning.

Heracles preferred wrestling, his favorite sport, as his primary method of giant disposal, and then he threw Diomedes to his hungry horses. For the less brawny hero, take the sneakier

A biscuit laced with sleeping potion
should tame Hades' guard dog

path by stabbing Diomedes in his sleep. Or, if that seems too cowardly, throw the sleeping giant to the horses, as the movement of being carried should give him a chance to wake and defend himself. Either way, to tame these horses, you'll want to feed them a one-course meal of their master. After all, to placate a normal horse, you give it an apple; in the heroic world, just scale up your thinking.

Once these man-eating horses are satiated, they should pose no problem. Really, on a full stomach, who'd put up a fight? Once your equine opponents finish devouring Diomedes, bind their mouths to keep them from having you for dessert. Then tie them together and bring them home. Hopefully, it's not a long trip as these wild horses get rowdy when their stomachs being to growl.

✦ CAPTURE CERBERUS ✦

TASK DIFFICULTY: ☠ ☠ ☠ ☠

Sometimes, your task seems impossible. Remember Hades' pet guard dog? In the discussion of the lands of the dead, you got a few tips for getting past this three-headed puppy. If you are sent to fetch him and bring him to the land of the living, you'll want to ask permission first, as you did with the Ceryneian Deer. You really don't want to be on Hades' bad side. Again, a personal sacrifice usually wins a god over.

Once you have Hades' permission, use any of the tactics we've gone over, such as lulling the dog to sleep or feeding him a biscuit laced with sleeping potion. If you opt to go this route, remember that a sleepy Cerberus will be a lot of dead weight to carry. Heracles kept the frisky pooch awake and wrestled him into a set of collars and a leash. (He's got three necks, so you've got to keep the collars from getting tangled.) But Cerberus didn't come willingly, which made Heracles' journey back a *lot* slower. Finally, watch out for his venomous slobber. Each bit of froth that drops on the ground gives rise to aconite, a deadly plant that can harm the mortals you're aiming to protect.

⇾ SEIZE THE GOLDEN FLEECE ⇽

TASK DIFFICULTY: ☠ ☠ ☠ ☠ ☠

The Golden Fleece is a much-desired item with a strange history: Long ago, there was a flying golden ram that was somehow a child of Poseidon. (If you think that's weird, remember that the Cyclops is also the son of Poseidon, so there's no telling what can happen.) This ram, being an altruist, saved two young children from being sacrificed by their cruel relatives by flying them to safety. On the journey to freedom, the little girl, Helle, fell off the ram's back into the ocean. (That part of the ocean—thereafter called the Hellespont—was named after her.) Phrixus, Helle's brother, was luckier and delivered in one piece to Colchis, where he thanked the flying ram—by killing him and sacrificing his innards to the gods. Phrixus then skinned the creature and kept its golden coat as a symbol of good fortune for his new kingdom. Any territory blessed with this item will be prosperous, so it's an accessory you'll want to own.

These days, Aeetes, the current king of Colchis, holds the Golden Fleece. A dragon guards the coveted item, and several tasks must be completed before he'd even think about handing it over. But it could be your lucky day, because Aeetes has a beautiful and brilliant daughter named Medea. And if you remember to comb your hair and wash your face, she'll probably fall for a handsome hero like you. She knows a thing or two about magic and, because she's hitting a rebellious stage, will likely help you in your quest against her father—as long as you promise to be faithful. Forever.

Chiron Enterprises does not recommend lying. We are not responsible for any oath taken with Medea or its consequences. We recommend that you do not break your word. Trust us, you will regret it if you do.

The ever-clever Medea will help you get through each task with flying colors, but the lessons you've learned thus far are also essential. Think of capturing the Golden Fleece as your first quiz.

Task #1: Just Plow Through!
The first of your tasks will be to plow a field with fire-breathing oxen. Review my advice on handling this type of animal in Chapter 7, the Not Your Average Menagerie section.

Task #2: Sink Your Teeth Into It
Next, in another feat with an agricultural twist, you will need to sow the teeth of a dragon into a field. From the seeds will spring an army of warriors. Defeat these men as instructed in the Earthborn Warriors section of Chapter 9.

Task #3: Rock-a-Bye Dragon
Finally, you will need to slip past yet another sleepless dragon. You can easily accomplish this with the many methods discussed for lulling an insomniac to sleep. Or, simply go after it with a potion spray, created with Medea's magical abilities.

Once the dragon is defeated, grab the Golden Fleece and get out of Colchis as fast as humanly possible. King Aeetes never planned for anyone to succeed in these tasks and will be enraged when he realizes you have his precious Fleece.

Shortly after the first edition of this guide was released, a young hero by the name of Jason sailed off to Colchis and grabbed the Fleece and Medea for himself, rendering the tactics here obsolete. As such, any hopeful heroes who want the Fleece will be able to grab it on their home turf. On the other hand, you may have to go through Medea. Chiron Enterprises takes no responsibility for any and all accidents involving Colchian sorcery.

→ PICK THE APPLES OF THE HESPERIDES ←

TASK DIFFICULTY: ☠ ☠ ☠ ☠ ☠

At the far western corner of the world, a blissful garden tended by beautiful nymphs awaits the daring adventurer. These evening nymphs cultivate Hera's orchard of golden apples. Hera hired a three-hundred-headed serpent, named Ladon, to guard the trees. Like most of Hera's guards, this ever-alert beast is a total insomniac. With so many heads, he never rests! To sneak past him, you'll need to stay awake at any cost.

The apples are an appealing prize, with uses beyond snacking. They're so shiny they can aid you in distracting a girl, as Hippomedes did in his footrace against Atalanta. And these juicy snacks have even been known to kick off decade-long wars.

How 'bout dem apples? Pretty powerful, right? I bet you're itching to get your hands on them—and here's how. To retrieve the apples, you've got two options. You can go the standard route and slay the guard (lull him to sleep as you did Hera's other sentinel, Argus). Or, to spice things up, use delegation (a great skill that will serve you well in your future career as ruler of a kingdom). Delegation works best when you offer to trade jobs. Just make sure you're able to do the guard's job yourself!

When Heracles went to the garden paradise, he befriended Atlas, the Titan who holds up the sky. Heracles offered to take

The Golden Delicious Decade of Battle

Eris, the goddess of discord, kicked off a war at the wedding of Peleus and Thetis, when she offered a golden apple to the goddess considered the fairest. Paris, a Trojan prince, was given the task of judging who among Hera, Athena, and Aphrodite should win the prize. Of course, each goddess bribed the judge—Hera offered vast political power, Athena offered strength and skill in battle, and Aphrodite offered him the most beautiful woman in the world. When—big surprise—Paris went with Aphrodite's bribe, there was a catch. Helen of Sparta, the world's most beautiful woman, was already married to Menelaus. But Aphrodite made good on her promise, and Helen changed her name to "of Troy." When Menelaus returned home to find his wife missing, he gathered all of her Achaean suitors, who'd vowed to help him rescue her. The Achaeans launched their thousand ships, and the rest, as they say, was history. Or rather, the rest, as they say, was epic.

117

over his job for a while if the Titan would face the dragon and fetch the apples. Of course, not being a Titan, Heracles couldn't have held up the sky for long. What's more, once Atlas got the heavens off his shoulders, he found himself enjoying the new-found freedom and was reluctant to go back to his old post. Because of that, the next step in Heracles' quest was crucial. (Make sure you're a good liar or you'll never be able to pull such a trick off. Otherwise, you, too, will be crushed under the prover-bial sky.) When Atlas returned, Heracles asked Atlas if he would relieve him from his sky-holding duties while he found a pillow for his neck. This way, Heracles explained, he could continue his work for Atlas more comfortably and for a longer period of time. Once Atlas was planted beneath the sky again, Heracles took the apples and took off before Atlas realized he had been tricked.

Remember: No matter how strong you are, there's some-thing to be said for making a quick getaway!

⊰ GOOD DEEDS ⊱

A hero's life isn't just about slicing and dicing for trophies and loot—even though that's the best part. Many heroes adopt a truly altruistic demeanor. And just because they're nice guys doesn't mean that they're wusses. Some of the most successful do-gooder heroes are totally badass.

I'm not talking about small stuff either, like lending grain or helping a neighbor fix his roof. A hero's good deeds tend to take place on a larger scale. For example, instead of helping a friend find his lost dog, you could bring his dead wife back to life. In return for the guy's superb hospitality, Heracles helped his pal Admetus by literally wrestling Death for the return of his beloved wife, Alcestis. That's right—he fought mortality just to do something nice.

→ I WOULD DIE FOR YOU:
ALCESTIS AND ADMETUS ←

Ordinary mortals don't usually get a chance to escape the clutches of the underworld, but Admetus was an exception. The story goes like this: At one point, Zeus grounded his son Apollo and forced him to live as a servant to mortals for a year. Apollo ended up working for Admetus's family in Pherae. Admetus turned out to be such a kind master that Apollo granted him a gift: Admetus would not have to die at his appointed time if someone else would volunteer to die in his place. At first, Admetus couldn't think of a better gift. But when his death day rolled around, he found that no one was willing to go to Hades in his place—except for his loving wife, Alcestis. After a lengthy speech in which Alcestis told Admetus to take care of the kids and never stick them with any kind of stepmother, especially not an evil one, she breathed her last breath. Admetus was understandably upset and soon began to quarrel with his father for not dying in his place instead. Had Heracles not stepped in, the whole family would have fallen apart!

→ PROMETHEUS: A REAL CULTURE HERO ←

Sometimes performing a good deed means righting a past wrong. At the beginning of time, the Titan Prometheus was punished by Zeus for helping mankind with their fireplaces. Because Zeus was feeling merciful that day, he tied Prometheus to a rock and sent a giant eagle to peck out his liver over and over again. When Heracles learned about this, he thought Prometheus had gotten the raw end of the deal. It was an

119

unusually harsh punishment for breaking the divine rules by being helpful to humans. Fully in touch with his do-gooder side, Heracles traveled all the way to the Caucasus to kill the big bird and free mankind's benefactor. Normally, Zeus would've been pissed at this thwarting of his divine will. But, since Heracles was his favorite son, Zeus was proud of his boy's strength.

Bringing fire isn't the only way Prometheus helped humans out. He's also the reason humans are allowed to eat meat! Back when gods and humans established the first sacrifice, each had to choose the portion of an animal that would be theirs for the rest of time. Prometheus pulled a bait-and-switch. Hiding the bones of the animal in appealing-looking fat, while putting the meat inside the disgusting intestines, he laid both options before Zeus. Zeus went for the prettier package, and ever since humans have had meat on the table. Next time you dig into a juicy steak, thank the Titan who got it for you!

These tasks are just a few of the many ways a hero can help mankind. Fame isn't always about the kill; sometimes it's about your character. But then again, I don't want to discourage killing, as it is fun and helps make the mortal world a safer place.

120

Lesson Learned

Fame isn't always about the killing; sometimes it's about the kind of person you are. (But then again, killing is fun too, and in its own way helps make the mortal world a safer place!)

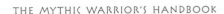

CHAPTER 11

GIVE WAR A CHANCE

A HERO'S CARNAGE

At this point in our lessons, you should be fully equipped to deal with any monster or madman who crosses your path or guards something desirable. But roaming the world's forests is not necessarily for everyone, and sometimes you'll find more excitement a few towns over. In that case, add to your heroic legacy by signing up for a war.

War makes sense for questers who prefer glory without all of the hiking. Besieging a town or city lets you quickly prove your valor, gain some loot, and take home some women as well! However, as both Achilles and Odysseus learned when they attacked Troy, not all wars are a quick-fix for your reputation. The Trojan War—fought between the Trojans, ruled by the wise and prolific King Priam, and a loose alliance of Greek kingdoms—lasted for a decade! While this war mostly entailed the standard hero-against-hero fighting with mortals trading blows and insults, even the gods got in on the action eventually.

⚛ THE TROJAN WAR ⚛
WHERE DID THE GODS FIT IN?

The battlefields of Troy became the ideal hot spot for the gods to act out their domestic disputes while helping their favorite mortals. If you ever find yourself in a similar war, you'll need to know which gods are on your side and which of them are fighting for the enemy. It's also best to avoid attacking a god in battle if at all possible, even if you have the help of a god who doesn't like him. For one thing, they're immortal, so beyond a simple scratch you'll only end up wounding their pride. Second, they'll be able to get you back in particularly nasty ways later. Diomedes managed to best Aphrodite in battle, but later arrived home to find that his wife had locked him out of the house and found herself some new boyfriends. Just payback from the goddess of love. Unable to return to his kingdom,

Wars of the Weird

War may sound completely mundane, but sometimes it has a taste of the supernatural. Ever wanted to battle a river? During his most famous rampage of the Trojan War, Achilles fought the river Scamander. Be careful, though—nature wields power! Achilles only survived because the gods intervened. With the help of the fire of Hephaestus, the river backed down and Achilles continued on his rampage.

Diomedes was forced to establish a number of cities in Italy before he could finally get his life back.

To give you an idea of how things played out during the Trojan War, here's a breakdown of which gods played for which team.

Team Achaea

Athena and *Hera* sided with the Achaeans, as they tend to favor that particular geographical location. They were also pretty sour after losing the beauty contest over the golden apple to Aphrodite, so they teamed up against Paris's hometown.

Thetis also sided with the Achaeans, out of loyalty to her son Achilles, as did *Hermes* and *Poseidon*.

Team Troy

Apollo had always been closely connected to the royal family of Troy. He once tried to date Cassandra, one of King Priam's daughters, and even though the love connection didn't work out, he still sided with the Trojans. When the Achaeans offended one of Apollo's Trojan priests, he sent a plague to make their lives miserable. Because Apollo fought for Team Troy, so did his twin sister, *Artemis*.

Aphrodite also sided with the Trojans, as Paris had always been one of her favorite mortals. (His designating her as the fairest goddess on Olympus only strengthened their friendship!) Of course, *Ares*, god of war and Aphrodite's long-time boyfriend, always liked to tag along wherever she went, so he ended up fighting on the Trojan side as well.

On the Sidelines

Zeus remained neutral in the conflict. If he had taken sides in this one, it would have shaken Olympus so hard it would now be known as a quarry instead of a mountain.

War always requires smarts in addition to strength, so any good hero needs to know battlefield strategy if he wants

Gotcha! How Odysseus Rooted Out Achilles

Achilles was something of a child prodigy when it came to the old wartime slice and dice, and because of that, the Achaean generals were dying to have him on their side for the Trojan War. Once he began his drag act on Scyros, however, none of them knew where to begin looking for him. Odysseus, however, had a hunch that Achilles was hidden somewhere among the daughters of Lycomedes, but he had to find a way of proving it. Figuring Achilles was bored spinning wool and would jump at any chance to show off his manliness, Odysseus arrived on Scyros with multiple chests of jewelry and a modest assortment of weapons, claiming they were gifts for the residents of the palace. Lycomedes' daughters immediately ogled the jewels, while Achilles fidgeted awkwardly in a corner of the great hall, trying not to lunge for the sword. Achilles may have pulled it off had Odysseus's sidekicks not pretended to attack the palace at that very moment. In response to their war trumpets, Achilles was swiftly on his feet. Ready to defend the palace, he seized a spear and shield, and from that point on, it was obvious how terrible he was in a dress. His true gender revealed, Achilles joined the war against the Trojans.

124

to excel. The Trojan War is a good teaching tool for this. Evidently, there was a whole checklist of items needed before the Greeks could take Troy.

→ BRAINS OVER BRAWN ←

While Achilles is hailed as the best hero at Troy, Odysseus truly deserves that honor. Even though Achilles killed the prince Hector in the ninth year of the war, weakening Trojan morale considerably, it took Odysseus's tactics to ultimately light the Trojan funeral pyres. Now, here's a role model for the thinking man! To plan a strategic conquest, any hero in training should try to emulate Odysseus's cunning craftsmanship. Earlier in the war, one of Odysseus's most successful strategies was his night raid on the Trojan camp. While the men of Troy were dozing, Odysseus and his best friend, Diomedes, snuck into the camp. They stole some fantastic horses but also managed to capture a Trojan spy who provided valuable tactical information.

By capturing the spy Helenus, a Trojan seer, Odysseus learned exactly what he needed to acquire in order to win the war. As is obvious from so many stories of heroics, prophets can have a pretty sadistic sense of humor. Helenus's list included:

- ☐ **The Palladium, a heavily guarded statue of Athena from within the walls of Troy**
- ☐ **The bones of Pelops, the grandfather of Odysseus's leader Agamemnon**
- ☐ **Achilles' son Neoptolemus**
- ☐ **The bow of Heracles (as well as its current owner, Philoctetes, who wasn't exactly going to be compliant in coming)**

While this sounds like a daunting list, Odysseus took it upon himself to get it done.

☑ Task #1: Swipe the Palladium.

Odysseus understood that desperate times call for desperate measures—in this particular case, theft. He and Diomedes snuck into the enemy camp, disguised as beggars, and wormed their way through a secret passage until they emerged safely on the streets of Troy. After that, stealing the Palladium was child's play, and the Achaeans were that much closer to victory. Keep in mind that Odysseus and Diomedes worked extra hard on their disguises, which prevented them from being discovered by the Trojans. If you want to be as excellent a tactician, it pays to be a master of disguise.

☑ Task #2: Recover the Bones of Pelops.

Odysseus arranged for the remains of Pelops to be sent to Troy via overnight delivery by Hermes, the package carrier of the gods who was on their side. In this case, Odysseus caught a lucky break!

☑ Task #3: Find Achilles' Son Neoptolemus.

The next—and more difficult—task was hunting down Neoptolemus. He was born on the island of Scyros when Achilles was hiding there, disguised as a young girl, at the beginning of the war. Dressing in drag wasn't Achilles' idea. Thetis, his mother, didn't want him to die in battle, so she came up with a way to dodge the draft. Since Odysseus was also responsible for outing Achilles' true identity on the island—another clever trick—he had a good idea where to look for his son. Imagine how Neoptolemus felt when he learned the lovely lady in the palace was actually his father! The lesson here? Always remember your comrades' whereabouts. You never know when you may need Junior's help.

☑ Task #4: Retrieve Heracles' Bow.

Taking Neoptolemus with him, and planning to use the boy's wide-eyed innocence to his own personal advantage, Odysseus went back to the island of Lemnos where he had left Philoctetes ten years earlier. Philoctetes hadn't been watching where he was going when the Achaeans had left for Troy all those years ago and had been bitten by a snake while trespassing in a sacred precinct. The wound that resulted smelled like week-old tahini and what's more, his screams of pain were so loud that the army couldn't get a decent night's sleep. In the end, the Achaeans were forced to leave Philoctetes on the island with nothing but the bow of Heracles to help him survive.

Whatever Happened to Neoptolemus?

So much for Neoptolemus's boyscout tendencies. Some time after they reached Troy, puberty kicked in, and he grew up to rage in battle even more than his father. Neoptolemus got to be so bloodthirsty that, during the sacking of Troy, he butchered King Priam on an altar—not exactly the most diplomatic of moves, especially when the old man begged to be spared. Take this as an example of when things go too far—being a hero might get you out of a lot, but it won't get you out of everything.

Only a man with a slick tongue and quick wit like Odysseus—and a sweet baby face like Neoptolemus—could have convinced this abandoned hero to help the Greeks who had left him to die! Keep this in mind when you need to make amends for earlier mistakes.

→ GIFTS SOMETIMES COME IN STRANGE, EQUINE PACKAGES ←

Having gathered all the ingredients on Helenus's list, Odysseus was just getting started! He added the extra spice to the hummus with the most famous military maneuver of all time. You've probably heard about it already, but your old pal Chiron is here to give you the details. When Odysseus snuck into the Trojan palace with Diomedes on the hunt for the Palladium, he noticed Priam had quite a large collection of horse figurines. Keeping this information in the back of his mind, Odysseus realized that the best way for the Greek army to take Troy was from the inside. He had a huge hollow wooden horse built and made sure that there was plenty of space inside for the best members of the army—himself included, of course. Before even laying the trap, Odysseus spent hours with the elite warriors engaging in hiding-in-a-giant-horse drills, which included games and lessons such as "How long can you be quiet?" "How to be comfortable with less personal space," and "How to hold your weapons so that they won't stab your neighbor." Once he was sure that the men could succeed in each of those skills, he made sure everyone used the latrine before entering the infamous Trojan Horse.

When the horse was positioned outside the gates of the city, the next phase of the plan went into operation. Odysseus had arranged for the second-best liar in the army (after

Odysseus's hiding-in-a-giant-horse
drill paid off

himself) to convince the Trojans to accept the present, claiming it was an offering to the gods. The Horse was brought into the gates. Once the sun had set, the Greeks sprang into action. Well, by *sprung*, I mean, they quietly got out of the equine structure, stretched their legs and backs, took a few practice swings, butted helmets to get psyched, and *then* they sprang into action, slaughtering the Trojans. Details, details.

Plan Your Own Surprise

Since the horse trick was such a success, you may wish to try another animal when constructing a soldier-filled gift for your raid.

Perhaps a cow to Hera or a bull to Poseidon—always make sure you match the animal to the god. If you are fighting against the Persians, an elephant is an animal that could hold quite a large army.

And when sneaking an army in through a statue as an offering to the gods, size does matter. Think about it. The Trojan Mouse would not have been nearly as successful.

130

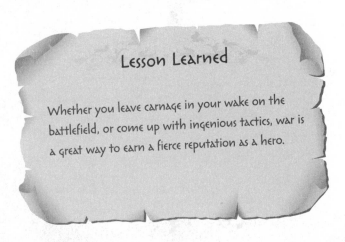

Lesson Learned

Whether you leave carnage in your wake on the battlefield, or come up with ingenious tactics, war is a great way to earn a fierce reputation as a hero.

HANGING UP

YOUR HELMET

CHAPTER 12

HOME SWEET HERO

SETTLING DOWN FOR THE LONG HAUL

Since you've just begun your heroic career, you're probably not thinking about retirement plans—you want to enjoy your youth! Honestly, if you can't spend your days now outside, taking down monsters, and collecting mystical items on quests, when can you? But sooner or later the day will come when you'll want to settle down and live out the rest of your life peacefully ruling over some acquired kingdom and swimming through that loot you amassed from your quests. Ah, the Achaean Dream!

Even if you think it's not for you at the moment, relatives and in-laws may pressure you into it later. When that day comes, you'll want to be ready. For what, you ask? For all of the pitfalls that may catch you off-guard during your retirement. After taking down a few winged serpents, you probably think there's nothing you can't face, but take it from your old pal Chiron—the psychological monsters of midlife crisis are even worse. That's why I've compiled this list of cautions for young heroes who will one day be leaving the business. Pay attention to me now, and it should save you some tragic twists in the future.

> Chiron Enterprises takes no responsibility for young heroes if Fate already seems to have it in for them. Young heroes should note that they are likely to be favored by the gods.

Let's not think too far ahead, though. After all, my next lesson is on modes of heroic death. For now, let's focus on all the ways to prevent you from growing bored once you've hung up your helmet.

❧ WEDDED BLISS? ❧

Once you get to a certain age, marriage seems like a normal enough thing to consider. But remember—as a hero, you're living in a world that isn't normal, and that goes for the realm of marriage. While it may seem like a good idea to have someone with whom to share your estate, it can be hard to find your soulmate.

→ HEROES GETTING HITCHED ←

In your quests abroad, you're going to encounter something even more terrifying than the fiercest of monsters—very beautiful, very clever women. Or, in some cases, very beautiful, very accident-prone women. The socially awkward among you might be wondering how you can catch the attention of these babes, and that's fair.

But you're in luck. You're a hero and, therefore, quite an irresistible specimen of manhood. Impressing the ladies should be a piece of cake—just give the object of your affection your dead monster count and she'll be whipped in an instant. Your word should be enough; no need to show her tangible evidence of your prowess. Pulling Medusa's head out of a bag may seem impressive, but remember, it'll turn anyone who sees it to stone. . . . You are looking for a girlfriend or a wife, not a new statue for your palace courtyard, right? Plus, even if they don't literally petrify people, most monsters look pretty gross. Try flowers instead.

As long as you stick to some of the social niceties of dating, your quests should provide plenty of opportunities to find a new girl. Here are some of the methods that have worked for other heroes:

Option #1: Whisk Her Away

In your travels, you're going to be meeting lots of girls who'd like to see something other than the four walls of the palace. Why not offer one of them a tour of the world? She'll thank you for getting her out of the house—but be careful, her father might not feel the same way! True, some fathers will be perfectly fine with your marrying their daughter as long as you ask permission first, but in the event they aren't, make sure your ship can beat his.

You could also kill her father to get him out of the way, as Pelops did to Oenomaus, in order to marry his daughter, Hippodameia. On the other hand, it could have negative repercussions, especially if by killing her father you're repeating the

135

pattern of overly creative violence that contributes to your hereditary curse. (To refresh your memory of Pelops and his descendants, see my notes on *Atreus, the House of.*)

Option #2: Win Her in Battle

This is a particular favorite of the heroes of the Trojan War, and many an Achaean general found a companion among his captives. There are, however, a few drawbacks associated with this method. For one, there's no guarantee that the girl you like will like you back, especially after you've just sacked her town. Second, there'll be a lot of competition between you and your allies. Anyone who ranks higher than you may feel he has a right to your girl, whether or not his contributions to the war effort are at all equivalent to yours. If you think this won't happen, think again—it happened to Achilles when Agamemnon

Greece's Most Eligible Bachelorettes

NAUSICAA: This princess of Scheria likes long walks on the beach. She once wanted to pair off with Odysseus, but now she's waiting for the next great hero to wash up on shore.

ISMENE: The one living princess of Thebes, she's looking for a shoulder to cry on after losing most of her family to a civil war. Could you be the lucky guy?

MEDEA: After Jason and then Aegeus, she's now single. But only for guys who are willing to risk the crazy. Who knows? She could be your next adventure!

took his girlfriend, Briseis, away. But if you excel at warfare, you can get your girl back by going on strike and refusing to participate in battle. Sit in your tent and sulk until enough of your allies have died that they want you back. For good measure, make it all about honor. After all, your higher-ups have violated your honor by trying to steal your girlfriend.

Once you've taken a time-out from the war, they'll soon be sending an embassy full of your allies to get you back into battle. They may even offer you gifts. (Or bribes, depending on how you choose to look at it.) Who knows? You might get your girlfriend back *and* score some sweet new tripods in the process.

Option #3: Beat Her in a Footrace or Some Other Athletic Event

Sometimes the aforementioned tomboyish types hold contests to see who is worthy of their hand in marriage, and anyone they beat in these contests is SOL. If the girl you're after falls into this category, start training right away. Don't underestimate her just because she's a girl—in fact, if she's good at what she does and you're desperate to marry her, devise a way to cheat. Suck up to the goddess Aphrodite, and she may give you a little help. Sometimes she even provides shiny golden apples to throw in the girl's path as a distraction.

However you find your bride-to-be, know that every type of girl you meet has some advantages for your cause. Some women you'll meet are helpers, who brew just the right potions for placating sleeping dragons and angry fathers. Others make you look good just by being rescue-able damsels in distress. Not only that, they're all hotties, and most of them are princesses, placing them within your acceptable dating pool now

137

that you've discovered your divine and/or royal lineage. There is a catch, however. . . .

While the ladies you meet on your quests may seem like marriage material, don't settle down with one right away! Many a hero has been brought down in his retirement by the wrong choice of a treacherous wife. To which you're probably thinking that you'll just avoid marrying a girl who's clever enough to scheme against you. Easier said than done. It's not just the clever ones you have to look out for. Don't you want a wife smart enough to resist the advances of other men who may try to court her in your absence? Or perhaps one smart enough to tell the difference between a poison and a love potion?

To add to those difficulties, it can be hard to tell one kind of girl from the next, especially when your vision's been significantly impaired by the goddess Aphrodite. Knowing this, I've prepared a quiz to help you be a little more objective in understanding your chosen partner. (No cheating!)

1. Jot down your answers:

α = Alpha
β = Beta
γ = Gamma

2. Match your totals to the key found at the end of the quiz.

Are You Married to a Tragic Heroine?

Chiron Reveals the Mysteries of Women

QUESTION 1: What does your girlfriend do in her spare time? This can provide insights into her personality, as well as her special skills. Your girlfriend's hobby is . . .

α Multitasking. She brews potions and makes clothing in an attempt to please me. She says she may end up combining these activities someday, but I'm not sure if I should be looking forward to it.

β Brewing and/or using mysterious potions to even more mysterious ends. I'm not exactly sure what goes into them or what they do, but she's nearly inseparable from her cauldron at times. If I ask her, she tells me she's just mixing cosmetics.

γ Weaving clothing and blankets. She's even made some for me and my family.

QUESTION 2: What's in a name? Just about everything. Chances are your girlfriend's parents had some idea of her nature when they called her what they did, and paying attention to the meaning of her name could give you some helpful hints for the future. Your girlfriend's name means …

α Man-slayer. 'Nuff said.

β Terribly, wickedly clever. Perhaps more clever than you? Be careful!

γ It's not clear, but it has something to do with needles and thread. Those are girl things, right? So that should be safe.

QUESTION 3: Time to consider the in-laws. When considering a prospective candidate for marriage, you should always evaluate how a potential spouse fits in with your family. In addition, think about your relationship to her family, and what hers is like in general. Which of the following best describes your respective family situations?

α Her family would be *all right*, but it seems as if they're just a bit cursed after that boar went rampaging through their land and her mother killed her older brother after her brother killed her uncles. Plus, you're not supposed to be engaged to her—her father had the strange idea of fixing her up with some ugly, uncouth river god. Your own family's pretty weird as well, so things will probably work best when you stay away from both.

β Her folks don't particularly like you, especially after you lifted stuff right out of their backyard and she dismembered her little brother on your behalf, but she'll take your side anyway. She'll also take your side against your own family, to the point where she'll even do away with your nasty uncle to help you out. In short, she's loyal but perhaps a bit of an extremist about it.

γ Despite the antics of one or two of her wild cousins named something like Helen and Clytemnestra, things run pretty smoothly, and she doesn't exactly follow their example. Her dad is okay with you marrying his daughter, and she gets along with your folks just fine as well. Everybody wins!

QUESTION 4: We've already pointed out the importance of intelligence when choosing a spouse. How would you rate your selected damsel's intelligence? Be honest.

α While she isn't entirely stupid, she's known for some lapses in judgment, especially when it comes to reading the labels on vials and *amphorae*.

β Smarter than you, though you don't like to admit it.

γ You're equal in intelligence. She comes up with the sort of plans that you might devise, and that's reassuring. It shows you can work together.

QUESTION 5: You return home, a little late from a hard day of questing. Your muscles are sore, and you're looking for a little sympathy. When you walk through the door, there's your damsel. How does she greet you?

α Gives you a sad, longing look, sighs, and then drapes a beautiful, soft robe over your shoulders.

β Screams at you for dawdling while she slaved over a hot stove, cleaned the house, and cared for the children. She says she's doing everything for you while you were out having all the fun.

γ Tests you to make sure of your identity and then welcomes you home. It's a bit frustrating at first, but it's very important to her that she remain loyal. She wouldn't want to cheat on you with a god in disguise!

✦ YOUR RESULTS ✦

Let's see which type of girl is right for you:

If you answered with mostly alphas (α), you, like Heracles, are with a Deianeira.

Deianeiras might seem low-maintenance at first. Initially, they're loyal, dutiful wives who are willing to go extra lengths for you because you saved them from some monster or other, as well as from more terrible marriage options. But watch out—Deianeiras are often too trusting, to the point of being a bit dim. If someone has it out for you, Deianeiras become pawns all too quickly!

The eponymous Deianeira, in an effort to spice up her marriage to Heracles, drenched a robe in what she thought was a *love potion* and sent it to her dear husband. Of course, the *potion* was actually a corrosive poison given to her by Nessus the Centaur, one of her husband's sworn enemies. Naturally, the moment the cloth touched Heracles' skin, it began to eat away at his flesh and burn him, which would have led to his ultimate and painful demise except that he jumped on a funeral pyre instead.

Oh, I forgot one thing: The name *Deianeira* means "man-slayer," which should have given Heracles a clue on day one.

If you answered with mostly betas (β), you, like Jason, are dating a Medea.

Initially, Medeas have their advantages. They're clever and effective women, and if they're smitten with you, they'll do what they can to help you on your quest. All they ask in return is that you marry them and stay by them. Sometimes, however, Medeas can be *too* helpful.

142

For instance, the original Medea first helped Jason gain the Golden Fleece from her homeland, but she had to betray her family in the process. If that wasn't enough, she left a trail of bits of her baby brother for her father to find as she and Jason made their escape. Talk about actions that will get you grounded for life! Once the newlyweds were safe in Iolchus, Medea wanted to help Jason again by solving his conflict with his uncle Pelias. So she spent some quality time in the kitchen with Pelias's daughters. Unfortunately, the secret ingredient in their stew was Pelias, and Jason and Medea soon found themselves in exile in Corinth.

By now Jason realized that his wife wasn't playing with a full deck, and besides, she'd gotten rid of all his problems. So he left her for the king of Corinth's daughter. Medea took revenge by killing his bride-to-be, his future father-in-law, and her two children by Jason, after which she made a quick yet stylish exit in a dragon chariot, furnished by her grandfather Helios, the god of the sun. There you have it: Not only do Medeas commit the most heinous crimes imaginable, but they know how to get away with it!

If you must date a Medea, be prepared to stick with her forever. She won't take lightly to breaking up, especially after all she's done for you.

Finally, if you've answered mostly gammas (Y), congratulations! You've found yourself a Penelope.

That means you've got very little to worry about. A Penelope has enough smarts to be interesting and a good companion, but she uses her intelligence to much less murderous ends than the Medeas or the Deianeiras. She probably thinks a lot like you do, and that's going to make you very compatible.

Penelopes are also known for their loyalty. In fact, the original Penelope, the wife of Odysseus, waited twenty years for her husband to return from the war in Troy. Though courted by more than a hundred suitors, she kept these eager bachelors at bay by a number of well-planned tactics equal in ingenuity to Odysseus's Trojan Horse. First, Penelope told these suitors that she'd choose herself a new husband after she'd finished weaving a funeral shroud for her father-in-law, Laertes. The suitors, figuring they could wait, fell right into her trap. Night after night, Penelope unraveled the day's weaving so that she couldn't finish the shroud before her husband returned.

When one of her maids ratted her out, Penelope switched to her backup plan and organized an archery contest. The suitors had to string Odysseus's rigid bow and then shoot a single arrow through twelve ax heads. While every suitor was eager to try, Penelope knew that only Odysseus could win this competition. Just like Penelopes themselves are the only ones who, in the contest to be the best wife, pass with flying colors!

After this quiz, you've probably got a better idea of your marriage prospects and what sort of girl is good for you. Since Penelopes are a rare breed, I suggest that you err on the side of caution when choosing a potential bride. In short, for all of you heroes, be careful when selecting a wife, and by all means try to stay on her good side!

Finally, just one last tip, sent in by our good friend Oedipus of Thebes: Don't marry any woman who bears a strong physical resemblance to you, especially if she's old enough to be your mother. You just never know!

✦ MARRIAGE FOR YOUNG FEMALE HEROINES ✦

Now, after that last bit of advice, I'm sure you heroines are feeling somewhat neglected by my narrative and are wondering what the future has in store for you when it comes to your love lives. Fortunately, for the young women who engage in heroic questing (and there are some of you Atalanta-wannabes listening, I know), my advice regarding marriage is much simpler: Don't do it, or at least try not to.

Marriage complicates everything, as evidenced by your young male counterparts. For you young heroines, however, it can be even worse. After all, many heroines are likely to have Artemis on their side because she is the tomboy of the goddesses. By marrying, they risk losing her favor and being left without divine aid. Not to mention, most husbands would prefer that their wives eventually retire from heroic questing and spend more time in front of the loom. This is especially strange considering how many husbands will claim that they were initially attracted by their ladies' skill with a spear or a bow and arrow, but then marriage does odd things to people.

That said, you will receive offers of courtship, and young heroes may present you with their own ideas of romantic gifts. This precedent was set by Meleager during the famous Calydonian Boar Hunt, when he presented the hide of the freshly killed boar to the Arcadian Atalanta both as a reward for her valor and in an attempt to win her affection. Since then, these sorts of gifts are beginning to catch on in the specialized circles where young men have regular interaction with socially deviant young ladies.

OTHER GIFTS TO WARM THE HEART
OF YOUR BELOVED

ARMOR: Particularly in her size, as it's so hard for heroines to find.

HUNTING SANDALS: For extreme sports rather than sitting around the garden.

AN ODE TO HER VALOR: Immortalize her deeds in song (or commission someone to do it for you).

Remember, no matter how much these hunting trophies warm your heart it's in your best interest not to be wooed by them.

You may want to spend some time thinking about how exactly to avoid a marriage, just so you're prepared for any eventuality. For example, try modifying a few of Penelope's tactics (see my description of Penelope's award-winning strategies in the previous section) and setting impossible standards for your potential suitors to achieve. You could also create contests that you know they can't win. Be very careful about loopholes, though, and try at all costs to avoid having suitors with Aphrodite on their side.

Let's explore some of the dangers of the latter.

Atalanta's Apples

A young Boeotian woman, coincidentally also called Atalanta—it may have been a popular name among royal couples that year—once decided to race against any hopeful young men. She claimed that should they want her for a wife, they'd have to beat her in a footrace first. This strategy worked out very well for her in the beginning, especially given Atalanta's talents in track and field. Suitor after suitor imagined himself to be the lucky guy to break the swift-footed maiden's winning streak, but without fail, each one was left in the dust.

That is, until a young man came along who utilized Atalanta's fatal weakness: She, like a magpie, loved shiny objects. And what could be more brilliant than golden apples provided by Aphrodite? The gossip lines call Atalanta's eventual racing-opponent-turned-husband by two different names, but whether he was Hippomenes or Melanion, he and the goddess of love were certainly on a first-name, you-scratch-my-back basis. Once this "Hippomelanion" decided that he wanted Atalanta, Aphrodite loaned him some special apples to toss in the girl's path. As Atalanta stopped to grab the enticing apples, one by one, she fell behind the few steps needed to give "Hippomelanion" the lead—and her hand in marriage.

Some reports say that Atalanta was pleased with her new husband anyway, and didn't mind so much. The newlyweds, however, were soon changed into a pair of lions by Zeus for violating one of his temples, so we were never able to get a clear answer from either of them other than some growling and a hungry stare.

147

Just Say No

In the end, Atalanta's predicament serves as another example of the dangers of marriage for young heroines. You're forced to give up your career, you risk angering your patron gods, or you get turned into some sort of beast without the power of speech. My pal Tiresias the seer says it may get better for you action girls someday, but in the meantime, know that settling down very often has drawbacks.

❧ CHILDREN ☙

THE PRODUCTION
AND MANAGEMENT THEREOF

Despite the doom and gloom I just predicted, one of the advantages of getting married is that your relatives and in-laws will no longer be able to nag you about doing so. Shortly afterward, though, they'll immediately begin to badger you about having children. Now, if you've made it through the marriage process and tied the knot without a hitch, you're probably thinking that children are in your future. After all, you've worked hard to build up a good name and a heroic legacy, and it's possible you want offspring to carry on that legacy once you're gone. Though you'll tell yourself that now, you may later wonder: Will my children continue my legacy, or will they steal it completely? Even worse, what if they get rid of *me*? Though it probably sounds paranoid at this stage of the game, the briefest look at the history of the universe shows that such worries aren't completely unfounded. You'll do well to remember the old adage: Just because you're paranoid doesn't mean that people aren't trying to kill you.

✦ CHOP DOWN YOUR FAMILY TREE ✦

Now, I hope you don't mind me borrowing a bit from that hotshot poet Hesiod's new bestseller, *Theogony*, but let's review the beginnings of the cosmos. One of the first couples to have kids was Father Ouranos, the sky, and Mother Gaia, the earth. Their kids included the tall and beautiful Titans, as well as the uglier Cyclopes, and some frightful, hundred-handed monsters. All was well for a while, save for the part where Ouranos didn't like any of his children. That, more than anything, put his relationship with Gaia on the rocks. Things got so bad that the Titan Cronus wounded his father with a scythe and usurped his power, becoming the new king of the universe.

Cronus and his wife, Rhea, gave birth to a new generation of gods, known as the Olympians. Of course, Cronus wasn't willing to let his sons and daughters repeat his own rowdy past, and he wanted to make absolutely *sure* they wouldn't become a problem. So, instead of confining the young deities to their rooms, he swallowed them whole and imprisoned them in his stomach instead. Rhea, having a much softer demeanor, didn't take kindly to such pre-emptive discipline. When she gave birth to child number six, better known to us now as Thundering, Cloud-Gatherer Zeus, King of the Gods and the Cosmos in Its Entirety, she replaced the drooling babe with a stone, which Cronus swallowed instead of his youngest son.

Like Father, Like Daughter

The goddess Athena's mother, Metis, would have borne a second child destined to overthrow Zeus, had Zeus not put a spin on his father's methods and swallowed Metis while she was pregnant with Athena. Athena, in turn, sprang fully grown, and wearing armor, from her father's head. As you'd expect, this caused Zeus the worst migraine ever. For his favorite and most loyal child, however, Zeus felt the pain was worth enduring.

Cronus swallowed a stone
instead of his drooling
babe, Zeus

Zeus (as he's called for short) was taken to the island of Crete and raised away from his father's infanticidal tendencies. Later, he returned home in disguise, made Dad sick enough to vomit forth his trapped older siblings, and challenged the Titans to war. Thanks to some help from Prometheus, the Titans were eventually defeated and Cronus was overthrown and killed.

At that point, Zeus was proclaimed the new king of the heavens, and he's been ruling ever since. Nowadays, Zeus remains in charge of Olympus because he's always on the lookout for power-hungry heirs. Considering his family history, it's difficult to blame him.

↦ RAISING LOVING CHILDREN, OR MAKING SURE THEY DON'T KILL YOU ↤

That said, taking into account that from the beginning of time, not even the *gods* could curb their children's patricidal instincts, starting a family should always be considered a dangerous undertaking, even for heroes. Even so, you may insist that you've discovered just the right parenting method that will keep your children from turning against you once they start hoping for that inheritance or for a raise in their allowance. Who am I to question your techniques? Perhaps things will work out better for you than they did for the immortals.

Nevertheless, I'd like to remind you that while not all accidents happen in the home, they're still statistically likely to involve a member of your family. Therefore, one of your children could be the cause of your death, and he or she may not even have intended it. Take the story of Aegeus, king of Athens, and his son Theseus, for instance.

Rearing Your Own Downfall

Aegeus was a young questing hero in his day, and Theseus followed in his father's footsteps when he decided to slay the Minotaur. Before Theseus left for Crete, he and his father worked out a way of best communicating Theseus's return. If he was successful in defeating the Minotaur, he'd raise white sails as his ship came back to Athens. If Theseus failed, his men would raise black sails, and Aegeus would know of his son's death ahead of time. As we've seen from our research, Theseus was indeed victorious against the Minotaur, calling for a white-sailed journey home. As bad fortune would have it, however, with all the partying he and his pals did on the ride back—including one rather wild stay on Naxos that damaged everyone's memory—Theseus forgot to change his ship's sails. When Aegeus saw the black beacons rising from the waves, he threw himself from the cliffs in shock and grief.

✣ DANGERS THE WHOLE FAMILY CAN ENJOY ✣

It's not just your own life that's put on the line when you have children—it's the lives of your children as well. Especially when they're young, your sons and daughters are easy targets for your enemies, like in these infamous instances:

HERA: Because Hera was mad at Heracles, she once possessed him with a rage so great, he killed his own children.

MEDEA: Medea, as we've mentioned before, got her revenge on Jason by killing his two sons.

TELEMACHUS: Telemachus, son of Odysseus, faced the threats of ambush and murder from the suitors looking to marry his mother Penelope in Odysseus's place.

THE MYTHIC WARRIOR'S HANDBOOK

Sometimes the gods can cause children to become liabilities in other ways, as well.

Iphigenia: Daddy's Little Sacrifice

The high king of Mycenae, Agamemnon, son of Atreus, was anxious to get to the war in Troy, but he couldn't set sail until the winds favored his fleet. Agamemnon consulted various seers and priests, and they all reached one grim conclusion: In order to sail to Troy, he would have to sacrifice his oldest daughter, Iphigenia, to the goddess Artemis. This is not an enviable position at the best of times, and Agamemnon's men were itching to go to war. What's more, when Agamemnon chose the option that put him in the running for the Worst Bronze Age Parenting Award (although, to be fair, he had a lot of competition, most of it from the members of his own family), he sealed his fate.

After the war in Troy, the moment Agamemnon crossed the threshold of Mycenae's Lion's Gate, his wife, Clytemnestra, pulled out the ax she had to grind over their daughter's sacrifice. Remember Clytemnestra? As we've said, she ground that specific ax right into Agamemnon's neck. From there, Agamemnon's son Orestes killed Clytemnestra for killing Agamemnon for killing Iphigenia.

Moral of the Story: Don't marry into the House of Atreus if you can avoid it. You'll never get the bloodstains out of the rug.

Worst Bronze Age Parenting Award

While Agamemnon might've been a pretty bad dad, he's only a runner-up in the coveted category of Worst Bronze Age Parent. And the nominees are. . . .

THE NOMINEES

OENOMAUS: He kept his daughter Hippodameia from dating anyone by constantly racing against her suitors in chariots.

LAIUS AND JOCASTA: These parents of Oedipus first crippled their son, and then left him to die on a mountainside.

MEDEA: Killing your own kids is a pretty good way to give yourself a dark reputation, though admittedly they may have lived through worse before she killed them.

THE WINNER

TANTALUS: Nothing like feeding your own son to the gods for an innovative and twisted way of ending the kid's life.

154

Now you can see why your parents might sigh and say, "You kids will be the death of me someday." You probably thought they were just being dramatic, but in the lives of gods and heroes, such a statement carries a literal twist. Whether your children outwardly rebel against you, or whether they're simply clumsy enough to deal you a fatal blow via the discus, they come with their own set of risks. Of course, this doesn't mean that children are always to be avoided. There is a chance they may be functional enough to carry on your legacy. To discover if they are, and to discover other events that may disrupt your bright future, you're going to have to start paying more attention to prophecies.

◄ PROPHECIES ►
AND THEIR INTERPRETATION

As we've been learning about the hazards of marriage and family life, you may be asking how it's even possible to predict such tragic twists of fate. This is why it's important to listen to what your friendly local oracle has to say. Oracles know the sordid past, the calamitous present, and the catastrophic future, and they can provide you with critical information on how to avoid those major life mistakes. Granted, oracles are often so obscure that you may not figure them out right away, even if you've been brushing up on your riddle-solving skills to defeat the Sphinx. Still the following tips should be an asset in dealing with oracles and the prophecies they deliver in your direction:

Tip #1: Find the Oracle That's Right for You.

Some oracles prefer to answer in the form of a cryptic poem, such as the Pythia at Delphi. Her answers are the most accurate, although they can be difficult to decipher until after whatever they're referring to has happened. On the other hand, if you're just looking for a simple yes or no, there are oracles who can provide that, too, such as Zeus's oracle at Dodona. Feel free to test a number of oracles by asking questions to which you already know the answers. A word of advice, however; do *not* boil a lamb and a turtle in a copper pot and ask the oracle what you've done. It may seem like the most bizarre activity you could choose from a list of highly obscure pursuits, but ever since King Croesus of Lydia pulled a similar stunt, it's become so well known that even amateur oracles will know what you're up to *without* using their second sight.

Tip #2: Don't Dismiss Wandering Prophets.

Some oracles are of the traveling variety, and by that, I'm referring to prophets. The most famous, of course, is my good friend Tiresias. This blind guy really can see the truth. Given the gift of prophecy by Zeus after siding with him in an argument with Hera, Tiresias travels the world warning people about their fates. He broke the news to Oedipus about his parents, he told Creon about Antigone, and he even warned Pentheus about his cousin Dionysus. If ever this guy wanders into your courtyard, do not, I repeat, do *not* think he is playing you. He is telling the truth, and you should definitely believe him.

Tip #3: If It Sounds Bad, It Is Bad.

When interpreting prophecies, keep your mind planted firmly in the gutter. More often than not, oracles have something to say about your relationship with your soon-to-be-appearing girlfriend. As King Aegeus discovered, even something as seemingly innocent as a wineskin could have a meaning unmentionable in polite company.

Tip #4: It's Always Best to Assume the Worst.

Oracles have a flair for the dramatic, so they'd prefer to predict a rain of blood rather than a simple springtime shower. If the prediction *sounds* bad (*hint:* frequent repetitions of

words like *death*), it probably is. If the prediction sounds innocent, it's still probably bad. Pay particular attention to a lack of
specifics. If the oracle says that a great empire will fall, there's a
good chance that the empire in question is yours and not that
of your enemy. Remember: No news is good news, and any
news could spell later catastrophes.

Tip #5: You Can't Avoid Fate.

Accept that any steps you take to avoid your fate may
cause you to walk directly into it, especially if the oracle tells
you something in a fairly clear and straightforward manner. When Oedipus was told he'd kill his father and marry his
mother, he did the responsible thing and left town—as it happens, it was the town where he'd been adopted. Little did he
know, he was en route to Thebes, the home of his real parents,
who, it seems, had heard the same prophecy and had done the
responsible thing and sent their child away. Looks like making two rights in an attempt to correct an oracle may result in
a right oracle! Given situations such as these, it's also benefi-
cial to know as many dirty family secrets as possible before
attempting to decipher a prophecy. You never know when it
might come in handy.

⇨ HOW DO ORACLES WORK? ⇦

Let's take a look into the art of prophesying. While it's
hard to say exactly how oracles do their job—every oracle
is different, after all—it's clear that prophecy is a gift from
Apollo. Those who have the ability to see the past, present,
and future are often some of his favorites, such as the Trojan
prince Helenus. Or, they may be his ex-favorites. At one point,
for instance, Apollo fell for the Trojan princess Cassandra—

157

Helenus's more unfortunate sister—and attempted to ask her out. For a god, though, Apollo's never had the best luck in his love life. Cassandra, like many other women before her, turned him down. Apollo was so distraught that he gave her the ability to make highly accurate prophecies. If that doesn't sound like a punishment, it came with a bit of a twist. Unfortunately, no matter how obvious the truth in Cassandra's prophecies, no one would believe her. If she said it was going to be sunny on a day when there wasn't a cloud in the sky, those near her would begin to seek shelter from the rain that was sure to come. Cassandra became increasingly distraught and often wailed and mourned for the city of Troy. In public, she wore black and sprinkled ashes over her forehead, which made her the embarrassing sort of relative you hate to have around on holidays. Imagine the looks on her family members' faces when she turned out to be right about the Trojan Horse. Unfortunately, this still didn't do anything for her credibility. Agamemnon brought her back to Mycenae as a captive, but he didn't listen to her when she warned him about his upcoming death.

Meet *the* Prophet

In addition to being the center of the world, Delphi has always been a sacred site for Apollo, ever since he slew the monster Python there in his youth and founded a shrine. While Apollo's luck with Cassandra and other women is poor, he does have a Best Friend Forever in the current oracular priestess at Delphi. This priestess is called the Pythia. In lieu of shouting down to her from Olympus—that amount of distance is tough even on divine vocal cords, and what's more everyone else would hear—Apollo communicates with the Pythia through threads of vapor that rise from a crack in the earth. It may sound strange, but it's certainly effective. When a questioner comes to Delphi, the Pythia inhales the vapors and receives an answer from Apollo in perfect hexameter verse. As a god of poetry and music as well as prophecy, Apollo can't help mixing his various lines of work. This no doubt keeps things interesting for the Pythia, who likes to keep her work flowing smoothly by reciting her answers rhythmically. Instead of repeating Apollo's answer directly to the inquirer, however, she first passes it on to the group of priests running her temple. The priests finally give the answer to the petitioner. Because of that, the answer often doesn't match up with the events in question. Think about it: If you say something to a friend, and he repeats it to a friend, and she repeats it to a first cousin twice-removed—well, soon you're going to have a completely different story. Still, don't blame any errors in prophecy on the Pythia; her direct line to Apollo makes her the most accurate oracle around.

> A final word of warning: Don't think that bribing the Pythia to say things in your favor will alter your fate. Just because everything she says is true doesn't mean that it necessarily works out that way. On the other hand, Apollo always appreciates a sizable donation to his temple, and that might just work out for you.

Keeping these tips in mind will not only help you make sense of some priestess's more creatively phrased predictions, it will also help you become a wise ruler. This is extremely important once you've finished with your questing. You will be expected to rule your kingdom well once you've returned there for good. When prophecies don't concern the gossip-worthy details of your private life, they may concern your kingdom's well-being. Often, they'll provide you with free, gods-given tips for everything from agriculture to war. The Greek generals, for instance, always kept priests skilled in divination on hand during the Trojan War to help them interpret various omens. Once they'd gotten over their initial resistance to listen to the gods, they were able to fight off the enemy and a plague sent by Apollo.

Just remember that no matter what happens, it's best to go with your fate, even if it's terrible. The gods have a habit of taking their own bad days and turning them into bad days for mortals, so you certainly aren't alone even if you do get a rather nasty prediction. As a final consolation, remember that those with the worst fates earn the right to complain about it—that is, as long as they wax poetic as is appropriate. There's nothing wrong with preparing for this eventuality, so you may want to practice your lamentations ahead of time. If you can think of a long, drawn-out metaphor to recite as you realize that you've accidentally cursed your own sons or daughters, or that you're about to die an ironic death, be sure to memorize it ahead of time. It will be a lot harder to compose these pearls on the fly when you're overcome by a grief as dark as the depths of Hades.

To brainstorm further, you may want to check out the work of my very talented student Achilles. *All Groans Up: How to Whine Like a Hero* is his ode for the doomed young man who feels as if he's gotten the short end of the kingly scepter. Likewise, any songs written by Orpheus after the first demise of his wife could serve as inspiration for your dirges. (Avoid the songs written after his wife's second death, however, as the critics at *Maenad Review* claim this as the point when Orpheus officially sold out.)

If you're following the example of Achilles and Orpheus, you could even try to play an instrument. Just imagine how great your laments will sound with the right chords to back them up! With a song in your broken heart and a lyre in your hand, even the pit of your heroic experience can be transformed into a moment of glory.

As much as you enjoy these snippets of splendor, there's a time and a place for them.

Lesson Learned

When contemplating the Achaean Dream, ask yourself: Is this really all it's cracked up to be? Sometimes the wife, the kids, the palace, and the dog ends up being a fatal formula. Just remember to pay attention to those oracles—they'll tell you what to look out for!

CHAPTER 13

REUNION TOURS

ALWAYS A BAD IDEA

My final suggestion for retirement seems so obvious it shouldn't even be an issue, and yet based on the experiences of past heroes, I find it best to pass this wisdom on to future generations. My warning is this: Retirement *is* retirement, period, end of epic, so enjoy that time for yourself and save some monsters for the next generation to slay.

Furthermore, if you're always running off in search of mystical objects, you'll soon run out of things to look for, and we'll all be out of a job. Think of it this way: Going out questing when your questing days are over distracts you from ruling that kingdom you worked so hard to get back from your nasty uncle. Why let all that hard work go to waste when you've earned your reward?

Not to mention, all of those domestic troubles with wives and children that we talked about in the last chapter are only exacerbated by heroes attempting to relive their youth.

Don't believe me? Heracles and Theseus didn't either, and look where it got them:

Heracles went out to sack cities, just as he did in the old days, and he thought a beautiful princess named Iole was just the right addition to the rest of his trophies. His wife, Deianeira, didn't agree, of course. That's what caused her to douse his robes in what she thought was love potion, as I told you earlier. If Heracles had just stayed home, he wouldn't have enjoyed the unique experience of his flesh burning slowly away from a deadly poison.

Moral of the Story: Next time you go out traveling, don't bring home a pretty princess as a souvenir.

→THESEUS AND PIRITHOUS IN THE UNDERWORLD←

In Theseus's case, he and his best buddy, Pirithous, decided to team up for one last tour of the Underworld. They figured it would just be one quick trip to see if they could carry off Persephone, wife of Hades, and they'd be back just before dinner. What could possibly go wrong? What Theseus didn't count on was getting stuck, quite literally, to an enchanted chair that would make it impossible for him to leave.

This may not have been too much of a problem for Theseus had life been completely in order back home in Athens. However, this was far from the case. Theseus's young wife, Phaedra, had given him up for dead, which technically he was.

Having forgotten the charms of her husband, she looked for companionship in her stepson Hippolytus (Theseus's child by the Amazon Antiope). Although the frustratingly chaste Hippolytus spurned Phaedra's advances, she got her revenge by hanging herself and leaving a note claiming that the affair was all *his* idea.

All of this transpired aboveground, until Heracles—no doubt entering through the revolving door installed just for him—found Theseus and hauled him out of Hades. Heracles wasn't able to rescue Pirithous, leaving Theseus bereft of a best friend. Theseus returned home to find his wife dead, supposedly on account of his stepson, and the entire palace in an uproar.

Hippolytus tried to defend himself against Phaedra's accusations, Theseus didn't believe him. Since exiling his son didn't seem to be punishment enough, Theseus called upon Poseidon to curse the boy as well. As Hippolytus drove away, a giant bull emerged from the sea, startling his horses and wrecking his chariot. He was killed in the crash, an event that never would have happened had he listened to a useful guide for monster slaying created by one particularly helpful centaur.

So, Theseus's little trip to the Underworld cost the lives of people who were very close to him—one of them at his own

Moral of the Story: If your family life is boring, don't take that as a sign you should liven things up by going to the Underworld. Trust me—things that are way too interesting will happen in your absence.

hands. If he'd stayed put in Athens, there's a good chance that this never would have happened. I hope that you can see through his example as well as Heracles' that questing after your time is up ends more often in disaster than it does in a satiated sense of nostalgia.

But perhaps you're not content to stay home and enjoy life after heroics. If that's the case, there may be a compromise between the life of the retired hero and the life of adventure. You can become an adviser to the next generation, which enables you to pass on the torch while still seeing a good deal of action from the comfort of your tent. Plus, giving good advice will raise your credibility as a wise ruler without having to become involved in too much nasty bureaucratic politics.

Perhaps the most famous retired hero-turned-adviser is Old Nestor of Pylos, who accompanied the Achaean generals on their expedition to Troy. A veteran of the old days with Heracles and Meleager, Nestor recounted a number of stories about the exploits of previous heroes to keep the morale high in Achaean camps. He also mediated the frequent disputes between Achilles and Agamemnon, although sometimes this proved a task too formidable for mortal men given both men's melodramatic tendencies.

⊰ WHEN WE INVADED TROY . . . ⊱

WE WALKED UPHILL, BOTH WAYS, BAREFOOT. . . .

If becoming a mentor to young heroes sounds good to you, plan your stories ahead of time so that you'll be able to tell them at the appropriate occasion. Memorize key phrases such as *in my day* to give your tales that special, grandfatherly diction. Soon you'll have a generation of wide-eyed youngsters hanging on your every word—or, if you're a mediocre storyteller, you'll at least put them to sleep and give them the rest they need for the big battle. Just remember to credit all of your best tips to the expertise of Chiron—the helpful Centaur who taught you everything you know.

Lesson Learned

If you worked hard to earn that nice time at home—remember, there's no place like it! Use your retirement to rest, not to relive old memories. Future generations will find you much more inspiring if you live to tell the tale. Or, if you'd rather go out with a bang, keep on listening for the best way to do it. . . .

167

YOUR BIG, FAT,

GREEK FUNERAL

IMMORTALIZING YOUR MORTALITY

DYING IN STYLE

T he best heroes are remembered not only during their lifetimes, but also long after they've left the mortal realm. Since we've already covered what you can achieve while you're alive, we're going to do everything we can to prepare you for that last, inevitable adventure: death. If this sounds a little morbid, don't worry. Death doesn't have to be the end. In fact, if you cast your knucklebones just right, you'll be just as active a hero even after you've shuffled off the mortal coil. I'll teach you how to prepare so that you won't be caught off-guard when that messenger brings your personal invitation to Hades' next open house.

The funny thing about death is that it can happen at just about any time, in just about any way. As a result, some deaths may seem to be a better fit for you than others. Keep in mind that a good death is all about being in the right place at the right time. For the younger hero, a death in the field—while slaying a beast or fighting a decisive battle—is the best fate you can ask for, especially if your sacrifice helps your comrades or city-state in some way. People will remember your deeds forever, particularly that last one, so plan your last words so they'll sound just right.

How to Die with Eloquence

Since there are so many ways to die, there are a lot of ways to express your sorrow as well. I've compiled a list, but you need to customize them to your particular situation. Feel free to experiment with the following styles when choosing your last words:

"I CALL DOWN A CURSE UPON YOU IN THE NAME OF ZEUS / POSEIDON / ET CETERA!"

Let's face it—if you've been stabbed in a vital organ and are bleeding to death all over the battlefield, you're probably going to be cursing up a storm anyway. Who better to curse than the enemy who landed you there? The gods are especially willing to answer such prayers, especially if they're already on your side, and it could mean a rather nasty twist to your opponent's fate.

"MY FRIEND / BROTHER / SON WILL AVENGE ME!"

Sometimes you've got a buddy out there who is close enough that he or she will be willing to kill your killer. Should this be the case, your friendship is truly something to boast about, even on the point of death. Remind your killer that although he got you, his time, *too*, is limited. What's more, predicting his death will save epic poets the trouble of having to fabricate the foreshadowing on their own. The pioneer of this style of last words was Achilles' best friend, Patroclus, who, after being fatally wounded by Hector, immediately reminded him that vengeance was on the way.

"I FORGIVE YOU."

Every once in a while, you run into one of those ironic deaths where someone close to you causes your downfall without meaning to do so. In this case, you may not want to hold a grudge for the rest of eternity, especially if it's against a family member. Even Hippolytus, who was trampled by his own horses as a result of his father Theseus's curse, forgave his old man before he left the mortal world forever. Think of it this way—if you want to come out looking like a nice guy, it's best to reconcile with those who have wronged you. Of course, it also helped that Artemis had promised Hippolytus a cult after his death, so maybe that put him in a better mood. Keep in mind that it's not *required* to forgive wrongs done to you—Heracles certainly wasn't complimentary to Deianeira in his own last words.

"PLEASE, PLEASE, PRETTY *PLEASE*, GIVE ME THE PROPER FUNERAL RITES?"

It may not sound heroic, but it's better than begging for mercy. Furthermore, if you've offended your opponent enough that he wants to kill you, he may want to *keep* killing you even after you're dead. Remember how Hector killed Patroclus? You'd better believe Achilles dragged Hector's body through the dust for days afterward, only handing him over when Hector's father, Priam, demanded it. Remember, too, that lost souls don't have the greatest sense of direction. Should yours go without a proper burial, you may be wandering around Earth for quite some time, unable to find your way to the Underworld.

"POETRY AND SONG WILL REMEMBER ME!"

Because as great as your deeds are, there's nothing wrong with dropping that one last hint to the writers of epic.

Another perk of dying young is that you'll look fresh and pretty for your funeral pyre, and it can't hurt to go out in style. Make sure you give those epic poets fodder for their hexameters.

Dying early, however, presents its disadvantages as well. You won't be around to reap the benefits of your performance on quests, and perhaps, even after all my warnings you really were looking forward to retirement. Furthermore, dying later in life gives you more options. You can still go out fighting in an intense final battle, but it's now also considerably less of a problem to die in your bed. If you're choosing the second option, make sure you've taken the time to be a wise and effective ruler of your particular kingdom so that your people will remember you for something more than your skills at combat. If you can leave your kingdom to a promising heir, that's just another leaf in your victory crown.

I would advise choosing *one* heir for the job—when Oedipus abdicated in Thebes, he failed to specify which of his two sons would be in charge. Rival brothers Eteocles and Polynices at first agreed that they'd each rule the kingdom every other year, but anyone who's ever tried the same method of sharing toys with their brothers and sisters knows how well *that* tends to work. Pretty soon Thebes was torn apart by civil war, both brothers were dead, and everyone else was miserable as well as they fought over the funeral rites. Only their youngest sister, Ismene, profited in the end; she sold the rights of her sordid family history to the tragic poets. This could spread the suffering to even more unlucky souls in the end, as our pal Tiresias predicted. Many generations of young scholars were forced to hear about the crusades of Ismene's sister Antigone, again and again.

⚜ WHEN WHAT DOESN'T MAKE YOU STRONGER KILLS YOU ⚜

Let us return, however, to death in the more general sense. Let me repeat, death is an unpredictable thing, so you may face an end that could be considered random, undignified, or otherwise unsuited to the legacy you've established for yourself. As much as such a demise sounds extremely, well, lame, don't let it bother you too much! After all, you're in good company with many of the heroes found in this book. Let's take a look at how the end of their lives played out:

LOOK OUT BELOW!

Jason was hit by a falling piece of the *Argo*, his trusty ship. To add insult to injury, his wife, Medea, called it ahead of time,

Attention, heroes in training:
A poorly aimed arrow can
lead to your demise

as she flew away on her dragon chariot and left him behind for good. Take a note here: It's probably best to leave the ship in the harbor; you'll have enough loot from your quest to display.

CURL UP INTO YOUR OWN DEMISE

Heracles, as we've discussed before, was eaten alive by the poisoned robe given to him by his wife, Deianeira. Not only is a robe thin and flimsy compared to the impenetrable hide of the Nemean Lion, which Heracles handled just fine on his own, but the feeling of one's flesh burning away isn't exactly a picnic either. So, avoid sudden fashion changes.

A LONG WAY TO FALL

Theseus was pushed over a cliff by one of his enemies. He didn't see it coming, and there's nothing that's quite so annoying as not being able to fight back. So always keep an eye on your surroundings and never let your guard down, no matter how old and famous you get.

WATCH OUT FOR IDIOTS WITH ARROWS

Achilles was shot in the heel by the Trojan prince Paris and bled to death. You may think a fatal arrow to the foot fits right in for a valiant death in war, but think again. Paris wasn't exactly the most skilled militarily of Priam's children, given his tendencies to wimp out and desert during battle. Nor was he particularly clever. In fact, the only job Paris ever did right was judge beauty contests—and some would argue that his choice of Aphrodite for Miss Olympus, though technically correct, had consequences that made his decision a flawed one anyway. In short, Paris isn't the sort of guy you'd expect to take down Achilles. What's more, his aim was so terrible that he had to take the shot with Apollo's help. How embarrassing!

From these examples, you can see that you don't *always* need to go out on a good note for your legacy to endure. Just make sure you have the great deeds during life—and maybe people won't notice that, like Achilles, you stumbled on your way out.

Lesson Learned

Whether your death is blissfully poetic or painfully ironic, there's one thing it can't be—boring. Make sure you're planning ahead for that one event in your future we all must face someday.

CHAPTER 15

ON DEATH'S DOOR

IT'S A BEAUTIFUL DAY IN THE UNDERWORLD

Now that we've considered all of the options for your physical death, let's plan out your afterlife. That's right—a hero's work will never truly be done, and there are various choices for how to continue your career for eternity. Not to mention, there are all sorts of perks to being dead that you may not have initially suspected.

For starters, let's talk real estate. Remember when I went over the layout of the Underworld, and the delights of the Elysian Fields? Now I want you to think about moving in; completing your quests has given you the right to do so. Not only is the weather so pleasant it's literally to die for, but you'll be surrounded by your heroic buddies, as well as other famous figures. Have you ever wanted to hear Odysseus tell about the time he and his men outsmarted the Cyclops, or spar against Achilles? Now you can!

ACHILLES: Though he can tell you a lot about what he did in the Trojan War, he may also whine about what it's like to no longer be alive. Don't catch him on a bad day.

HECTOR: If you're keen on hearing the other side of the story, you can ask this Trojan son of Priam how the war went for him!

AJAX: Well, you can try and talk to him about his role in the war, but he's not so keen on conversation since he's started giving Odysseus the cold shoulder.

HERACLES: Though he spends most of his time on Mount Olympus, he occasionally takes a vacation to Elysium to hang out with his old heroic buddies.

HELEN: Yep, she's down here too! Why let being dead stop you from flirting with an attractive former queen of Sparta? Just don't let her husband Menelaus find out!

180

⊰ CUTTING ALL TIES? ⊱

THINK AGAIN!

Generally when people go to Hades, they cease to interact with mortals, but this doesn't have to be true for you. One way to extend your influence beyond the grave is by having your own heroic cult. While the hero cult doesn't provide all of the special perks found in godhood, it does give you a set of kooky powers for helping out mortals.

✦ PLAYING THE FRIENDLY MIDDLEMAN ✦

Since you'll be on a level between the gods and the mortals, you'll be much more approachable than Zeus, and as such, you're going to be hearing a lot of prayers. In gratitude, mortals will continue to pay you respect after you're dead, maintaining your tomb and leaving you offerings. Just because you've left the earth behind doesn't mean that your house has to be in disarray and that you can't enjoy the occasional snack.

The other benefit of having a hero cult is that your burial site will become hallowed ground. Oedipus, for instance, wandered away from Thebes after being blinded. When he died near Athens, he was buried outside the city, and ultimately his bones benefited the Athenians by resting in their soil. If you're notable enough, various city-states will be fighting like crazy to gain possession of your remains.

And hey—why not make the best of it while you're still alive? If you qualify, there's nothing wrong with hearing the cases of various city-states that want your remains and perhaps accepting a bribe or two on the side. You may even decide to hold an auction to see which city-state bids the highest for you. What better way to celebrate your popularity? Of course, there's nothing particularly moral in this course of action, but it might help boost your income. Remember, too, that after your death various kingdoms will be fighting for your bones anyway—sometimes going as far as to declare war—and at that point, you won't be able to profit from it.

Some city-states to keep in mind when choosing a tomb-site:

ATHENS: It's not Thebes!

THEBES: It's not Athens!

LESBOS: A home of poets, with an arts district and great nightlife

CORINTH: Fabulous ocean view!

SPARTA: Where you'll always get a warrior's respect

→BACK FOR MORE: HOW TO HAUNT←

Sometimes, you may not want to help other mortals. Perhaps you've had a rough time of it as a hero and suffered a lot to achieve greatness. In this case, you may choose to come back as a violent, demanding ghost. Nowhere could you find a crankier, more restless spirit than Achilles.

Achilles: Can't Get No Satisfaction

Although he can tell you a lot about what he did in the Trojan War, Achilles didn't have much luck finding and keeping a girlfriend. His first choice, Briseis, was taken by Agamemnon when he was forced to give up his captive Chryseis at the request of her father. (Agamemnon, some suggest, subscribed to the theory that since the two girls' names rhymed, one couldn't be that different from the other.) Later in the war, Achilles found a kindred spirit in the Amazon Penthesileia, but perhaps she was too much of a kindred soul. Both liked fighting so much that they had their first date on the battlefield.

182

As rotten as Achilles' luck with girls was when he was alive, you wouldn't think his love life could improve much after he died. That's where'd you be wrong. Achilles' spirit held a lot of pull among the Achaeans, and they never considered his ghostly demands unreasonable. Once the Achaeans had conquered and sacked Troy, they each chose one of Priam's daughters to take home with them. Not wanting to be left out, Achilles' ghost appeared to them and demanded the princess Polyxena as his bride in the Underworld. As a result, the poor young girl was sacrificed at his tomb. In the end, Achilles got his fair share of the loot even though he was dead.

✎ REACH FOR THE STARS ❧

If you don't end up gaining your fame in the depths of the earth, there's still the option of being immortalized in the skies. Instead of spending their afterlives in the Underworld, some heroes become constellations, brightly illuminating the night sky. Not only will you improve your reputation by being a friend to astronomers and sailors, but you'll also be even shinier in death than you were in life. Ascending to the great vault of the heavens, you'll be in the good company of many other heroes:

GET TO KNOW THESE RISING STARS

ORION: Orion was a hunting buddy of the goddess Artemis, and when he was killed fighting a giant scorpion, she requested that he be placed among the stars. The three brightest stars in his constellation make up his hunting belt.

PERSEUS: The first of our heroes now hangs out. You might recognize him by the way he holds his arm in a Y shape.

THE DIOSCUROI: The two brothers Castor and Polydeuces, inseparable during their lives, now shine together brightly.

PEGASUS: Bellerophon's trusty steed flew to great heights, but now he soars among the heavens.

CHIRON: Yours truly! Those of you who end up as constellations will have the benefits of my advice for all eternity.

Keep in mind that should you become a constellation, you're going to need to return to your career slaying monsters. For some reason, the gods have as much of a tendency to populate the skies with pests as with those helpful young folks who got rid of them during life. But don't worry too much—I've covered all the ways of dealing with these beasts right here in this guide. From the Nemean Lion to the dragon that guards the Apples of the Hesperides, you'll be able to take on each and every one of the nuisances you meet among the stars. Not to mention, you'll have sidekicks such as Pegasus to help you with your endeavors. For those of you who are looking to impress fair damsels, rest assured that ladies such as Andromeda and Ariadne will be there, too, marveling at your every move.

A hero's future,
in the stars

⛧ FEELING UPWARDLY MOBILE? ⛧

But perhaps simply being a ghost or a constellation isn't enough for you. Perhaps you're such an overachiever that you won't rest until you're at the top of the universe—and by the top of the universe, we mean Olympus.

That's right—if you've been a hero among heroes, then you have the chance to become one of the immortal gods. From then on, your life will be nothing but lazing about in the sunshine, feasting on ambrosia and nectar while listening to the melodious songs of the Muses, with no pain or disease to disturb you for the rest of eternity. Well, you are going to have to deal with some fairly intense family quarrels, given the tendency of the gods to fight over just about any detail of day-to-day divine living. Also you'll often be called on to solve the problems of mortals in a way that would seem implausibly tidy if it happened at the very end of a story. (There's a reason we call an ending like that a *deus ex machina*.)

Before you start aiming for divine status, is this something you want to be dealing with forever? Trust me, when I say *forever*, I'm not exaggerating. Forever isn't just a long time, it's the longest time there is.

✦ APPLYING FOR DIVINE MEMBERSHIP ✦

Of course, not just anyone can achieve divine status. First, there are a certain number of prerequisites if you're going to be admitted to Club Olympus. Zeus and Company don't just admit anyone into their little cohort; you have to have the proper connections. Specifically, I mean family connections. That said, if you don't have a parent who is a prominent god, you're not likely to find your place among the immortals any time soon. What's more, it's very helpful if your parent is Zeus. For some reason, the old Cloud-Gatherer isn't too keen on competition from his relatives' kids.

Second, if you're going to become a god, you're going to have to stop being mortal. Although this should be obvious, the loss of mortality is actually one of the most physically painful parts of becoming a god. The mortal parts of your body actually need to be physically removed and replaced by more divine material. The best way to get rid of a mortal body is to

---

Trial by Fire:
What Went Wrong with Demopohoon

Similarly, we could look at the example of young Demophoon, the son of the king and queen of Eleusis. When her daughter Persephone was kidnapped, Demeter felt the empty nest syndrome kicking in and decided that having a son was the perfect solution to the problem. Instead of simply giving birth to a boy, however, she decided to steal one from a mortal couple. Taking on the role of the child's nurse, Demeter placed him in the fire every day and burned parts of his mortal self away. Then she fed him nectar and ambrosia to make him immortal. This probably would have worked out, if Demophoon's mother hadn't entered the room and pitched a fit. This was understandable, since she saw a daft old woman throwing her baby into a fire. Just imagine the look on the queen's face, however, when Demeter revealed her divine status and her true intentions.

---

burn it, of course. Just ask Heracles—the one upside to having his flesh burned off by a poisoned robe is that it made his transformation into a god a little easier.

✦ BANQUETING WITH THE ETERNALLY BLESSED ✦

Speaking of nectar and ambrosia, they're going to be very important once you've acquired your brand-new immortal body and golden ichor flows through your veins instead of blood. These divine variants on food and drink are guaranteed to keep you going day in and day out, just like wine, bread, and meat do now. As you may recall, some lucky demigods were given ambrosia as an energy booster.

Unfortunately, you're going to have to kiss your favorite foods goodbye. Gods don't eat the same kind of food that mortals do—it's against the rules, after all. Of course, nectar and ambrosia are apparently far superior to anything you might consume as a mortal. Rest assured that even if you miss your old favorites, you'll be able to satisfy your cravings somewhat by inhaling the vapors from sacrifices. Every time humans barbecue for a festival, the smoke finds its way to you and the rest of the gods. Just because you've gone on to another plane of existence doesn't mean you can no longer enjoy the occasional aroma of a good steak. (Remember: All gods love steak!)

✦ AND THAT'S NOT ALL. . . . ✦

There are other major life changes to take into consideration when becoming a god. You may, for instance, find a new spouse. Heracles, for instance, was given Zeus and Hera's daughter as his third and final wife. He was one lucky hero: Since his new wife was a god, he couldn't go mad and kill her, and since he'd become a god, she couldn't kill him either. Plus,

188

this truly fortunate divine hero managed to get quite the hot young wife. A hero can't do better than to marry a goddess named Youth!

ॐ PUBLICITY ॐ

THAT'S AS LASTING AS OLYMPUS

From here, I know you're thinking, there's no other place to go. After you've become a god, what could possibly be left? But here's the catch—as much as you do, as many monsters as you slay, as many miles as you travel in a quest, as many cities as you found, as many songs as you compose about your forever-doomed love life, no one is going to care if they don't hear stories about your adventures. That is why to be the most remembered hero of all time you're going to have to make sure people tell your story.

Let's think about the heroes we've covered in these lessons. By now, you may have realized that they weren't always perfect, and they didn't always do things as well as they should have. Could Heracles have thought his actions through once in a while? Of course. Should Achilles have learned to control his temper? Certainly. Did Jason do anything on his own at all? Absolutely not! Without Medea or Hera to help him along, he never would have made it to Colchis and back. But all of these heroes had one thing on their side that allowed them to stand the test of time—publicity. And what better publicity than stories so exciting they're told at every banquet?

Before you leave the mortal world, identify someone to relate your story to others in one way or another.

→THE POWER OF THE POP SONG←

Earlier, I mentioned that the musically talented among you, like Orpheus, may want to compose songs about the trials and tribulations of your life. But these songs probably won't be the same with someone other than you—probably some rhapsodic poser—singing them. Nobody likes a cover artist.

→THE VITALITY OF VERSE←

Before you die, you may want to make sure there's some poet ready to record a version of your life that everyone can sing. Now, of course, there are popular choices like Homer and Hesiod, but if they're booked, you may want to identify a bard with more time on his or her hands. You never know—you might just find the person who tells your story better than you ever could. Remember, too, there's more than one way to tell a story, and some styles may suit your quests better than others.

The Eternity of the Epic

Are you looking for a long, drawn-out tale related in an elevated poetic diction? Perhaps something that can be told in episodes? Then you're going to want to have your story—like Achilles' in the *Iliad* and Odysseus's in the *Odyssey*—told as an epic. An epic may take a long time to get through, but for all that you've done you're going to need that extra space.

Told Again Through Tragedy

Maybe you're one of those heroes who, like Oedipus, has been beaten up by fortune. If you want to look noble and enduring despite having your reputation dragged through the mud, try having the story of your life narrated in a tragedy. What's a tragedy? Well, it may not be a popular genre *yet*, but my old friend Tiresias tells me that in another hundred years, tragedies will be as big as television and movies (Tiresias says that these other means of telling tales are going to be pretty big once they're invented). Tragedies are always performed in groups of three, so in addition to tragedies about you, there'll also be tragedies about those horrible family members who make your life more difficult.

✦ STANDING OVATIONS FOR SATIRE ✦

Do you want to show posterity your sense of humor? Show up in a few satyr plays! Tiresias tells me that they're going to show these after tragedies, when crowds are in need of something that's less depressing. Satyr plays can show all the happy endings that result from your quests. For instance, there's the one about Heracles wrestling death and rescuing Alcestis, wife of his good friend Admetus, which will cheer up audiences after they've watched Oedipus blind himself or Theseus curse his son to death. Not to mention, if you add in a few scenes of Heracles singing and tipsy, the audience may even relate. Think of it this way: The crowd that laughs with you never turns against you.

✦ MEMORIALIZED IN A MASTERPIECE ✦

Don't forget that a picture's worth a thousand words, too! As long as you're planning to immortalize yourself in a verbal fashion, there's something to be said for making sure that artists are on your side, too. There will be those people who don't have time to sit around listening to an epic or a tragedy, but certainly they can glance at a statue. Find a sculptor whose style works well for depicting your particular body type, and commission him or her to bring you to life in marble. Be sure you're able to stay still for a long time, though; you're going to

have to strike a noble pose as you model for your chosen artist. Remember that many sculptors chose to depict heroes in
the nude. If you're hesitant about being seen without clothes,
now would be the time to lose those inhibitions. Keep in mind,
though, that after working out during your questing, your
torso should be ripped. In the end, you should have nothing to
worry about.

Don't Stop at Sculptures

Spreading your image doesn't need to stop at museum
pieces, either. Your image can appear on things that people
see every day. Perhaps your story will be depicted on the side
of a temple or a coin. Or perhaps you'll even make it onto the
vases, plates, and drinking cups that everyone keeps in their
household. Think of it this way—soon, people will be thinking of you every time they take a sip of wine. Simply because
you're fighting for the common good doesn't mean you can't
make a little money merchandising. Of course, if you're feeling
generous, you may want to share some of the profits with your
old pal Chiron. He's done so much for you, and it costs money
to train the next generation, after all.

✦ . . . AND EVERYTHING AT ONCE! ✦

Of course, as a hero, you probably excel at multitasking,
so there's no reason you can't show up in these different types
of stories and portraits at once. What better way of showing
the diversity of your personality to future generations? We've
already pointed out that Heracles was a marathon-style hero,
who fought just about every monster he could. In his afterlife,
he's also been in just about every kind of story there is, bringing laughter, tears, and inspiration to audience after audience.

There's a *reason* he's so famous, even today, and it's that you can find him pretty much anywhere.

⛧ A NEW KIND OF IMMORTALITY ⛧

But the most wonderful thing about being mentioned in stories and carved into the sides of buildings is the inevitable ripple effect that results from all of that public exposure. Human beings can never get enough stories about heroes, and generation after generation will want to put their own spin on your particular story. Tell one story, and someone else will tell another story based on it. Soon another will follow, and then another. Tragedies will follow epics, brief but powerful poems will follow tragedies, wall paintings and frescoes will be inspired by these media, television and movies will appear further down the line, and then the Internet . . . that's another one Tiresias says is going to be great. Perhaps, watching someday from the stars or a haunted tomb or Mount Olympus itself, you'll be able to see for yourself.

193

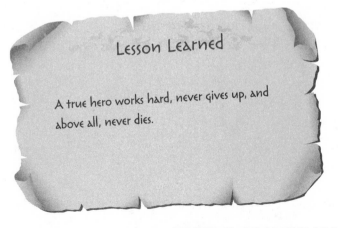

Lesson Learned

A true hero works hard, never gives up, and above all, never dies.

APPENDIX A:

CHIRON'S NOTES TO THE GODS

For those of you who were too busy daydreaming about your future quests while in religion class to pay attention, I have included this appendix of the various deities you may encounter in this handbook and in the real world to help you. Be sure to pay attention to their jobs, as well as their personal preferences, so you may enlist their aid as needed. As you know by now, gods respond well to gifts catered to their very specific, very discerning tastes. This little guide should give you some hints on where to do your shopping!

✦ APHRODITE ✦

OCCUPATION: Goddess of love.

SPOUSE: Hephaestus.

LOVERS: Ares, Anchises, and the list keeps going on. . . .

CHILDREN: Terror, Fear, and Eros (with Ares), Aeneas the Trojan hero (with the mortal Anchises).

BIRTHPLACE: Cyprus.

STRENGTHS: She herself is beautiful. In fact, she's the embodiment of beauty itself. But maybe you don't want a girlfriend that's as high-maintenance as a goddess. If that's the case, never fear—Aphrodite is also great at matching you romantically with other gorgeous women. And remember, nothing gets a fair maiden to help you quicker than a crush on you! Aphrodite's aid is therefore useful when you require some help from the local princess on your quest. Just know that her love spells are very strong and not to be used light-heartedly. Make sure you're okay sticking with the maiden in question for life!

WEAKNESSES: Really self-absorbed—but with legs like that, who's blaming her? While she knows how attractive she is all too well, be sure to compliment her constantly anyway. Also when playing matchmaker, she's not big on monogamous relationships—for herself or for others! Make sure to check on the marital status of the girl you court; you really don't want to have her husband's army following you home.

✦ APOLLO ✦

O((UPATION: God of music, prophecy, archery, philosophy, and reason. You'd think a guy like that could get a date, but . . .

SPOUSE: None. His girlfriends keep turning into trees (Daphne) or going crazy (Cassandra).

(HILDREN: Asclepius, the god of medicine, by the mortal woman Coronis.

BIRTHPLACE: Delos.

STRENGTHS: Like his twin sister Artemis, Apollo is an excellent archer. He also gets in touch with his cultured side by being creative in poetry and classical music. If you're looking for a well-rounded career, Apollo could cover a lot of bases for you. Moreover, Apollo is the guy in charge of oracles—which can be both useful and detrimental to any hero. Sure, there are advantages to knowing your future—but what if your future isn't so sunshiny bright?

WEAKNESSES: Since he is not as successful as his father Zeus at being the ladies' man, I don't suggest that you bring up ex-girlfriends in conversation. Mark my words; he will make you listen to his whiny breakup ballads for days. Of course, since he's divine, they're actually very *good* whiny breakup ballads—but trust me. Just about anything gets tedious once it's overplayed.

→ ARES ←

OCCUPATION: God of war.

SPOUSE: None—he's too busy making out with Aphrodite to really look for one. Not to mention, most goddesses aren't interested in a guy who's so into bloodshed.

CHILDREN: Terror, Fear, and Eros (with Aphrodite).

BIRTHPLACE: Thrace.

STRENGTHS: Fearless, and capable of stacking up quite the body count. If you want your war to have impressive statistics, he may be the guy to go to.

WEAKNESSES: Ares is impulsive, bloodthirsty, and always up for a fight—even on those (admittedly rare) days on Olympus when everyone would rather relax than quarrel with each other. Since mindless slaughter isn't really as effective as strategic maneuvers in battle, you might want to turn to Athena for help conquering a city instead.

Note: As we've mentioned in the chart which plotted out the relationships of the gods, Ares is extremely pliable to Aphrodite's will, so if you've got her on your side, there's a good chance he may end up tagging along anyway.

✦ ARTEMIS ✦

OCCUPATION: Goddess of the hunt, mistress of animals, and the protectress of children. Also helper of mothers giving birth, so you can thank Artemis for bringing you into the world alive.

SPOUSE: NEVER! This girl is focused on her career.

CHILDREN: I repeat, NEVER!

BIRTHPLACE: Delos.

STRENGTHS: Physically strong and independent, with quite keen aim when it comes to her arrows. She defends both herself and those under her protection such as children and wildlife. Just because she's a protector of animals, however, doesn't mean she won't engage in a little hunting—her favorite hobby, and one at which she truly excels. If you're looking for a hunting buddy who will keep you challenged and on the trail, look no further! Just keep in mind the one little catch. . . .

WEAKNESSES: Artemis hates men. Though there have been special exceptions to the rule, such as Theseus's young son Hippolytus, you may not want to be quite so zealous in your own Artemisian worship, especially since it means giving up dating. The heroines among you will have more luck with her—though you, too, will have to be careful! You're going to have to be content with the idea of never settling down. Because marriage causes women to lose their freedom, Artemis opposes it, and the nuptially inclined will find themselves losing her support on their quests.

OCCUPATION: Goddess of military strategy, wisdom, the city of Athens, and also arts and crafts.

SPOUSE: NEVER!

CHILDREN: I repeat, NEVER! Well, maybe she'll adopt in rare cases. Erichthonius, the first king of Athens who was born from a union of Hephaestus and Gaia, was Athena's adoptive son.

BIRTHPLACE: From the forehead of Zeus on Olympus. No kidding.

STRENGTHS: Daddy's little girl, she almost always has his support. Having Athena on your side is a good indication that Zeus's help follows. She even gets to wear his aegis, a special shield with a Gorgon's head on it, which creates fear in the minds of her enemies. As far as her attitude goes, she's very intelligent and rational in most cases. She also excels at military strategizing, so keep her on your side when your enemies have employed the help of Ares.

WEAKNESSES: Though too rational for most emotions like compassion, Athena does have her occasional favorite mortals. If you embody her personal traits, like Odysseus did, she will help you in every way she can. However, if you're not the cleverest ram in the sheepfold, you're much less likely to earn her sympathy. What's more, never claim that whatever Athena can do, you can do better. Last time a woman named Arachne claimed she wove better than Athena, she ended up a spider.

200

→ DEMETER ←

OCCUPATION: Goddess of grain and agriculture.

SPOUSE: Not married.

CHILDREN: Persephone, queen of the Underworld.

BIRTHPLACE: First time: not known. Second time: regurgitated from her father Cronus's stomach. Yick. This also goes for Hera, Hestia, Hades, and Poseidon.

STRENGTHS: Controls crop productivity. Useful to beseech when ruling your kingdom, but not really needed on your quest, unless you're growing the food to take with you ahead of time. You'll also want to make sure to travel to places she favors, if you want to be welcomed with a big feast upon your arrival.

WEAKNESSES: Very protective of her daughter, Persephone, who spends ⅔ of the year above ground and ⅓ of the year as queen of the Underworld. She is willing to let the world die of famine if she doesn't get her way—talk about a hunger strike!

✦ DIONYSUS ✦

OCCUPATION: God of wine, madness, theater, and raw emotions.

SPOUSE: Ariadne, sister of the Minotaur, whom he met during her lovely extended vacation on the island of Naxos.

CHILDREN: None.

BIRTHPLACE: Mount Pramnos on the island of Ikaria, from Zeus's thigh. He would have been born mortal, but his mother Semele was struck dead with a lightning bolt while pregnant. Baby Dionysus had to be sewn into Zeus's leg to incubate a little longer—with the upshot that he ended up born a god!

STRENGTHS: Created wine, the juice of life and the life of a party. He is always up for a good time and is great at shaking up a dull day. You're certainly going to want to have him around the next time you cut loose!

WEAKNESSES: As a god of wine and madness, he's not very good at being helpful. Dionysus is just too busy partying to care about the larger picture. What's more, if he comes to you and you don't acknowledge him as a god, you're likely to end up as a dolphin—or worse.

→ EROS ←

OCCUPATION: God of love.

SPOUSE: Psyche.

CHILDREN: Delight.

BIRTHPLACE: Crete.

STRENGTHS: Handsome and causes people to fall in love. Can help you out in finding a spouse with which to run your future kingdom. On the other hand . . .

WEAKNESSES: He can always make you fall in love with the wrong person! What's more, he's usually simply doing the dirty work for Aphrodite in setting people up with each other. And as I mentioned before, Aphrodite isn't too picky in pairing up couples, and you may end up with someone who's already married or otherwise incompatible with you.

203

↔ GAIA ↔

OCCUPATION: Earth goddess.

SPOUSE: Uranus.

CHILDREN: The Titans, the Cyclopes (some of them), and the Hundred-handers.

BIRTHPLACE: Born from Chaos, a huge gap in time and space.

STRENGTHS: Since she is the earth itself, she is capable of aiding any of her children who touch the soil. She also can generate earthborn warriors already equipped with metal weapons from her own ore.

WEAKNESSES: Gaia's just as capable of producing monsters as she is of producing things that'll help you. If you get on her bad side, she's likely to produce your next worst enemy!

→ HADES ←

OCCUPATION: God of the Underworld.

SPOUSE: Persephone.

CHILDREN: None.

BIRTHPLACE: See the entry for Demeter.

STRENGTHS: Rich with the wealth of the Earth. Rules the underworld firmly with few visitors' passes even being granted. Also, a dog lover, as he is the owner of the three-headed puppy Cerberus.

WEAKNESSES: Feels left out from the livelier crowd at Olympus, and can spend some time brooding in the gloom of the underworld. He also can be very deceptive to get what he wants. He is not easily persuaded, but can have his mind changed by his lovely bride. If you want to be on Hades' good side, make sure you have Persephone's approval first.

→ HEPHAESTUS ←

OCCUPATION: God of the forge.

SPOUSE: Aphrodite.

CHILDREN: Erichtonius of Athens—though this kid in particular was raised by Athena.

BIRTHPLACE: Olympus.

STRENGTHS: A fantastic metal worker, he makes only the finest tools and armor, such as the shield of Achilles. He also will play the court jester to break up the larger fights amongst the gods, having quite the sense of humor. Moreover, he is craftier than he lets on, and enjoys tricking the gods who anger him.

WEAKNESSES: Has a bad leg, so he can't maneuver easily, and is often mocked for this by his divine relations. He's a bit sore about it so if you want his help I suggest you ignore his malformed limb.

206

→ HERA ←

OCCUPATION: Queen of the gods, as well as the goddess of marriage.

SPOUSE: Zeus.

CHILDREN: By Zeus: Ares (god of war), Eris (goddess of strife), Hebe (goddess of youth), Eileithyia (goddess of childbirth). By herself: Hephaestus (god of the forge).

BIRTHPLACE: See the entry for Demeter.

STRENGTHS: Hera is powerful as the queen of all the gods, but not powerful enough to keep her husband in line. Still, she knows how to get around him and make things better for her allies when it counts. If you've got Hera on your side, she'll pull the strings to get you ahead.

WEAKNESSES: Despite being the goddess of marriage, she seems to not be able to extend that power over her own husband. Thus she is not a big fan of Zeus's heroic illegitimate kids, and will probably try to make your life more difficult. The only exception is if you accidentally help her out when she's on Earth as an old lady. That could change everything for her, but only if Zeus isn't your papa.

✦ HERACLES ✦

OCCUPATION: Hero turned god.

SPOUSE: Megara (killed by his own hand), Deianeira (killed by her own hand), Hebe (the goddess of youth).

CHILDREN: First batch by Megara (killed by his own hand), Hyllus by Deianeira, and the two twin minor gods Alexiares and Anicetus by Hebe. Not to mention a whole number of others whose descendants now flood the plains of Greece. . . .

BIRTHPLACE: Thebes.

STRENGTHS: Heracles' bravery, determination, and massive strength are what caused him to be the only hero to make it to the status of god. He may just have some friendly advice to help you out on your own quests.

WEAKNESSES: Heavy drinker and wife slayer. He also is a bit too proud to really help heroes follow in his footsteps. He can also be a little dim.

→ HERMES ←

O((UPATION: God of liars and thieves. Also works part time as a messenger god and escorts dead souls to the Underworld.

SPOUSE: None, yet.

(HILDREN: By the nymph Dryope: the faun Pan, the god of shepherds. By Aphrodite: the bizarre Hermaphroditus.

BIRTHPLA(E: Arcadia.

STRENGTHS: Hermes is extremely clever, crafty, and resourceful. He can trick anyone! He also enjoys messing up the plans of other gods, so if you are being persecuted by a deity, Hermes will most likely help you out.

WEAKNESSES: Since he is always running around, Hermes isn't very good at just sitting still doing nothing. What's more, while he can use his tricks to your advantage, if you aren't careful, the trick might end up being on you!

209

✦ HESTIA ✦

OCCUPATION: Goddess of the hearth.

SPOUSE: NEVER!

CHILDREN: None.

BIRTHPLACE: See the entry for Demeter.

STRENGTHS: Keeps out of the family squabbles by staying at home.

WEAKNESSES: Keeps out of the family squabbles by staying at home. So she won't be helping you out.

→ MUSES ←

CALLIOPE, CLIO, EUTERPE, TERPSICHORE, MELPOMENE, THALIA, URANIA, ERATO, POLYHYMNIA

OCCUPATION: Patronesses of the arts.

BIRTHPLACE: Pieria, at the foot of Mt. Olympus.

STRENGTHS: These nine sisters are quite the artists! Each covering a different aspect of the popular media, the Muses dictate how information gets out into the world. They won't help you on your quest, but they will help to immortalize your fame.

WEAKNESSES: They've got a bit of a reputation for being liars—just ask the poet Hesiod—and as such, some of the things that they say about your deeds may later be taken as a poetic fiction.

211

→ PERSEPHONE ←

OCCUPATION: Queen of the Underworld.

SPOUSE: Hades.

CHILDREN: None.

BIRTHPLACE: Not known.

STRENGTHS: Beautiful, and naïve during her childhood though she's starting to gain some experience now. Capable of changing Hades' mind.

WEAKNESSES: Her beauty and innocence caused Hades to choose her as his queen of the least lively realm, the Underworld. While out playing with her friends one day, Persephone was lured over to a narcissus, and it was here that Hades jumped out of the earth and whisked her off to his underground home.

✦ POSEIDON ✦

OCCUPATION: God of the sea and fresh water as well as god of earthquakes.

SPOUSE: Amphitrite (sea nymph).

CHILDREN: By Amphitrite: Triton the merman. By Medusa: Pegasus the winged horse. By the mortal woman Aethra: Theseus the hero. By the Cyclops Thoosa: Polyphemus, the most famous Cyclops.

BIRTHPLACE: See the entry for Demeter.

STRENGTHS: Controls the often-tempestuous seas, and as such can be a good ally when you're making a journey by boat. Believe it or not, he's also a god of horses, so you may want to invoke him while traveling by chariot, too.

WEAKNESSES: Prone to quite the temper. Don't get on this god's bad side, or you'll find yourself too far upsea without a paddle—literally.

✦ PROMETHEUS ✦

OCCUPATION: Champion for humankind, professionally angers his cousin Zeus on humans' behalf.

SPOUSE: None.

CHILDREN: None.

BIRTHPLACE: Not known.

STRENGTHS: Knows the future so he can hold that over Zeus's head. Also, supports mankind, giving them fire and civilization. However, he thinks in terms of the really big picture so he is less likely to help just one human.

WEAKNESSES: Picks on the most powerful deity, which turns out badly for him.

214

✦ THETIS ✦

OCCUPATION: Minor goddess of the sea—but just because she's minor doesn't mean she isn't worth paying attention to.

SPOUSE: The mortal King Peleus of the Myrmidons.

CHILDREN: Achilles.

BIRTHPLACE: Not known.

STRENGTHS: Quite the attentive mother, and knows how to play the Olympian power politics. Has Zeus on her side after she once saved his life, so possesses the ability to call in favors.

WEAKNESSES: Generally only helpful if you're her kid. What's more, Hera doesn't like her too much, so you risk getting the queen of the gods against you should you seek the aid of Thetis.

215

→ ZEUS ←

OCCUPATION: King of the gods as well as Manager of Lightning.

SPOUSE: Hera.

LOVERS: Too many to name.

CHILDREN: Too many to name.

BIRTHPLACE: Mt. Ida on Crete.

STRENGTHS: Highly powerful. His lightning bolts also prove to be a persuasive technique for motivation and getting his way.

WEAKNESSES: Can be a bit moody when he doesn't get his way. While he enjoys fathering the heroes, he won't help you out though.

216

APPENDIX B:

THE HERO HALL OF FAME

You've heard a lot about a number of great heroes through-out this book. However, following are the stories of the top five Greek heroes. Some use their brawn, some use their brains, but all of them make this job look very easy. Look to them for inspiration during your quests.

✦ PERSEUS ✦

Perseus's grandfather shipped him and his mom, Danae, off to sea because of some information an oracle told him. Grandpa Acrisius was warned that the little tot would overthrow him one day. So off he sent them. (You'd think a grandparent would *want* his grandchild to be successful.)

Mother and son landed on the island of Seriphos where a nice fisherman, Dictys, took them in. The fisherman's brother, King Polydectes, took a liking to Danae. But he wanted Perseus out of the way. So off Perseus was sent, again.

This time, Perseus was told to go a-questing. The king demanded that he fetch him the head of Medusa. This was a little more complicated than a simple slice job. First Perseus needed to get the monstrous lady's whereabouts from the Graecae, a trio of grey-haired sisters who shared one eye and one tooth between the three of them. Then he scored some helpful gear from Hermes and Athena. After succeeding in the beast's beheading, Perseus stopped by Ethiopia where he met his future bride, Andromeda. This poor damsel was being sacrificed to another beast, Ceto, because her beautiful mother Cassiopeia had boasted that she was more beautiful than some goddesses. Before going heroic on the water beast, Perseus negotiated a marriage contract with Andromeda's father, King Cepheus. Once those details were hashed out, he slew the monstrous sea creature and rescued the damsel.

With Medusa's head in one hand and the hand of his new wife in the other, Perseus returned to Seriphos to confront King Polydectes. The king wanted the head of Medusa so the king got the head of Medusa. Perseus used the monster's stone gaze on his stepfather. And Perseus's little revenge spree didn't end there—he went back to his grandfather's kingdom and "accidentally" hit him in the head with a discus, killing him instantly. Oops.

✦ HERACLES ✦

The son of Alcmene, Heracles is truly the greatest of all the heroes. He began his heroic acts as an infant, strangling the snakes that his goddess stepmother Hera sent to kill him. When that plan failed, Hera made sure that if he was going to live, he sure wasn't going to enjoy it. She placed him under the command of his cowardly uncle, King Eurystheus, who sent him on over a dozen quests after Hera made Heracles go crazy and kill his first wife Megara, and all their kids! The funny thing was, despite asking for all of these quests to be completed, he didn't seem to really want Heracles to succeed. Every time Heracles brought back evidence that another quest was finished, he hid in the nearest storage jar.

Now, each of the beasts and deeds of Heracles' quests can be found in Chapters 7–10, but to list them briefly: He killed the Nemean Lion, the Lernean Hydra, and the Stymphalian Birds. He then captured the Ceryneian deer, the Eurymanthian boar, the Cretan Bull, and Hades' pet Cerberus. He cleaned the messy Augean Stables, he rounded up the Mares of Diomedes, and the Cattle of Geryon. He stole the belt of the Amazonian Hippolyte, as well as the Hesperidean golden apples. In addition to these—as if they weren't enough—he helped Jason on his quest for the Golden Fleece, was a slave of Queen Omphale, rescued Prometheus, killed Giants, rescued a woman from the Underworld, and so much more!

Honestly, it's a good thing his wife got jealous of the new servant girl he brought home, and wound up accidentally killing him, or there would be nothing left for any other hero! But even death didn't stop his heroic tale. For all his good deeds, Zeus rewarded him with immortality and gave him a place on Olympus, as well as a beautiful wife, Hebe, known as an eternally youthful, good-looking babe.

☩ JASON ☩

Jason's parents actually wanted to keep their newborn alive. (Weird, huh?) However, his uncle Pelias had very different plans; he greatly desired to destroy his young nephew. Fearing this, Jason's mother Alcimede saved her baby by pretending that he had been stillborn. She then made the best call of her life, and sent her young son to be raised by the wisest, smartest, kindest, sweetest, most ingenious, most beloved tutor and foster parent in the world—me!

With his nephew out of the way, Pelias became paranoid over another rival. He had been given an oracle predicting that a single-sandaled man would be the death of him. Little did he know that the man who arrived on his doorstep clad in only one clog was his long-lost nephew, Jason. Being a good boy, Jason had lost his shoe when he helped an old woman—Hera the queen of the gods in disguise—cross a river. This was to be a good move on our hero's part. When Pelias attempted to get rid of Jason by sending him on a quest to find the Golden Fleece, the queen of the gods was actually helpful for once!

Hera helped set Jason up for his quest. She recommended an architect to build his ship the *Argo* as well as helped to gather all the heroes available to go with him on his quest, including Heracles, Orpheus, and Atalanta. On their journey to Colchis, the land of the Fleece, the crew encountered several obstacles such as the Harpies and the Symplegades. But thanks to the great heroic Jason, they made it to Colchis in (mostly) one piece. There he met the beautiful and crafty Princess Medea, who helped Jason in the various tasks that were necessary to gain the Golden Fleece.

Jason returned to Pelias's palace with the Golden Fleece and a new witchy wife in hand. And it was actually this new wife who had revenge on Pelias. She tricked his daughters into cooking Pelias in a stew. She promised him youth as a result of being the main ingredient, but it really caused him to be the main course.

Our two lovers then exiled themselves to Corinth, where they settled down and had a few kids. However, Jason's eyes strayed to the royal daughter of King Creon, and he couldn't help but propose. Medea, not really a fan of sharing her husband, didn't choose the usual route of passive aggressive behavior. Instead, she slaughtered their kids and his bride-to-be before flying off in a chariot drawn by dragons. How's that for an exit? Jason was left alone, and was eventually killed when a piece of the *Argo*, the ship from his adventurous youth, hit him on the head. A warning to all you heroes out there: You really should never take a nap under rotting wood.

→ ACHILLES ←

Achilles was one of my more tragic pupils. His mother, the sea nymph Thetis, was prophesied to bear a son stronger than his father, so Zeus—who had taken a fancy to her—passed her off to the mortal King Peleus of the Myrmidons. Apparently there was another prophecy to his name as well. Poor Achilles was fated to either live a long inglorious life, or die young but famous. For this reason his clever mother hid him on the all-girl island of Scyros, dressing him in drag, to avoid his being sent to fight in the Trojan War. But Odysseus—as you read earlier—found him there and dragged him to battle.

There, he just couldn't keep a girlfriend—either High King Agamemnon was kidnapping his most recent captive (a nice girl-next-door called Briseis), or Achilles himself was ending the life of Penthesileia, an Amazonian queen with whom he'd really hit it off. Problem was, both shared a love for killing their opponents in battle. Still, defeating her did add to his kill count even if it didn't get him a date.

221

After being truly awesome on the Trojan battlefield, Achilles was killed in his one weak spot, his heel. You see, in his infancy, his mother held him by the heel to dip him in the River Styx in order to make him immortal. All but that small spot was bathed, making it his only weakness. Paris, the biggest loser of all those Trojan flunkies, managed to get a lucky shot and pierced Achilles with his arrow right in the heel. What a shame to be hit from afar instead of going out in the heat of battle!

✦ ODYSSEUS ✦

Odysseus—the most clever hero out there—was the son of King Laertes and Queen Anticlea of Ithaca. He was a happily married man, wedded to the perfect woman Penelope with whom he had a son, Telemachus. But when the Trojan War engulfed all the best men from Greece, scouts came to Ithaca looking for able-bodied men to fight. Menelaus would stop at nothing to get his wife Helen back, and was willing to sacrifice all the men in his kingdom to do so. At first Odysseus attempted to disqualify himself from the draft by feigning madness. But when the other Greeks didn't buy his ruse, he went around dragging other heroes like Achilles into the mess, too.

During the war, Odysseus's strategic skills shone. He was famous for his various tactics and techniques rather than his brute strength or fighting skills. The most famous of all his ploys was the Trojan Horse. This sneak attack enabled the Greeks to finally end the ten-year war.

After the war he was forced to wander the seas for ten more years, a lesson in never angering the god of the sea, Poseidon. He hung out with nymphs, and battled Giants, Cyclopes, and witches! When he finally returned home, he found that over 100 men had taken up residence in his palace, all attempting to court the lovely Penelope. Athena—a huge fan of the cunning Odysseus—gladly helped take the suitors out with the trash. But Odysseus still had one last quest to fulfill. Tiresias had prophesied that the only way he could placate Poseidon was to bring an oar inland until someone mistook it for a fan. Then after a sacrifice to the sea god, Odysseus was able to live a long and happy life.

INDEX

225

❧ ABOUT THE AUTHOR ☙

Chiron the Centaur was a half-man/half-horse and highly respected tutor of many ancient heroes, including Theseus, Jason, Ajax, Heracles, and Achilles. Skilled in all the ancient fighting techniques and knowledgeable of the ins-and-outs of the gods and monsters that ruled the ancient world, Chiron was also known for his expert healing abilities as well as un-Centaur-like intelligence and peacefulness (both a result of his being taught by Apollo and Artemis). Born to the titan Kronos, Chiron gave up his immortality to save Prometheus and died in battle by Heracles' side. He once lived on Mount Pelion with his wife, Chariclo the nymph, and his four children, but he now resides in the skies as a constellation.

❧ ABOUT THE TRANSLATORS ❧

Erika Carlson is a native of Maryland where she is currently finishing work on her master's degree in Classics at College Park, but she considers Bryn Mawr, her undergraduate college, as her spiritual home. Like her favorite poet Ovid, Erika enjoys mining the mythic tradition to create stories of humor and pathos in her own writing. In addition to authoring her own Classics-based fiction, she also hopes to one day teach at the university level; that is, if she doesn't get picked up by the Tardis first.

Heather Day is originally a Jersey girl, who studied Classics at Wheaton College in Massachusetts before completing her master's degree at the University of Maryland where she taught Classical Mythology. She grew tired of students' bored stares and chose the option of mocking myths as a way to get some attention. She is saddened by both her students' and her cat's dislike of the Latin language. She currently teaches Latin to high school students in Pennsylvania, but still hopes to drive on the BBC television show, *Top Gear*.